D0457268

SCHMOOZING WITH TERRORISTS

SCHMOOZING WITH TERRORISTS

FROM HOLLYWOOD TO THE HOLY LAND, JIHADISTS
REVEAL THEIR GLOBAL PLANS — TO A JEW!

AARON KLEIN

WND BOOKS

SCHMOOZING WITH TERRORISTS
A WND Book
Published by World Ahead Media
Los Angeles, CA

Copyright © 2007 by Aaron Klein

Cover Design by Linda Daly

WND Books are distributed to the trade by:

Midpoint Trade Books
27 West 20th Street, Suite 1102
New York, NY 10011

WND Books are available at special discounts for bulk purchases. World Ahead Media also publishes books in electronic formats. For more information call (310) 961-4170 or visit www.worldahead.com.

First Edition
ISBN: 9780979045127
Library of Congress Control Number: 2007928664
Printed in the United States of America

10 9 8 7 6 5 4 3 2 1

*In memory of the victims of the September 11, 2001, terror attacks and the victims of Palestinian terrorism throughout the years.**

*A portion of the author's proceeds will be donated to charities associated with aiding terror victims.

In eternal memory of my Grandmommy, Marilyn Sacks, one of the strongest women I knew; and my Grandmom, Sima Klein, who dedicated her life to her grandchildren.

CONTENTS

ACKNOWLEDGMENTS

To Susan Roth, nothing I do would be possible without you. From this book to my reporting to my survival in the harsh, dysfunctional jungle that is the Middle East, I have you to thank. You've gone above and beyond. You are a gift from heaven and a true *Eshet Chayil* ("woman of valor") in every sense.

Thanks to my loving family for their unceasing support: David and Carol Klein; Miriam and Amir; Asher and Gila; Josh; Sara and Joey; Rebecca; Chaya; Gabriella; Aliza; and the bar mitzvah boy, Mendy.

Joseph Farah—my editor-in-chief, mentor, and occasional (Christian-leaning, Arab) "rabbi," words cannot express my appreciation to you and Elizabeth for all you've done in support of me and my reporting the last two years. Looking forward to working together for many more eventful years to come.

Many thanks to all the wonderful editors at *WorldNetDaily.com,* including the patient David Kupelian; Art Moore; Ron Strom; Bob Unruh; and Jay Baggett. Thanks to Shannon and Michelle! A special thanks to Joe Kovacs, the world "Title Champion," for his creative help in naming some of the chapters.

To my translator, Ali Waked, who risked his life to accompany me on these terror adventures. Thanks for putting up with my ever-changing requests and deadlines and for all the many ways you helped these past few months. Looking forward to working together on *Schmoozing with Terrorists—The Sequel!*

Thanks to my trusty researchers, including Ashley "The Skipper" Rindsberg, Miriam Waxman, Aaron Sichel, and Mikael Tossavainen.

A special thank you to Irving and Cherna Moskowitz and David and Rachelle Bronfman for their valued friendship.

ACKNOWLEDGMENTS

A shout out to the great folks at the *Jewish Press*, especially Jason Maoz and Avraham Shmuel Lewin; the editors of the *NY Sun*; and the staff of *Ynetnews*.

Thanks a million to all the great people at World Ahead Publishing, including Eric, Norman, Ami, and Judy.

And last but most certainly not least to all my radio host friends, I cannot possibly thank you guys enough! You've enhanced my reporting and enriched my Middle East experience in so many ways:

To John Batchelor, who gave me my first radio gig. You took a chance on an unknown kid who wandered into your New York studios one cold January evening. From being denied entry to countries to dodging Qassams to mixing up terror leaders to water sprinklers shooting into our radio equipment while broadcasting live from trucks on Gaza beaches, our many adventures together so far have been glorious.

To Sean Hannity for your help in getting out crucial stories and for being accessible despite your superhuman broadcast schedule.

To Rusty Humphries, my partner in crime—thanks for believing in me, for all the exposure and for not going nuts the many times I got us lost in the West Bank at two o'clock in the morning. We've wreaked so much havoc together I'm surprised an international law hasn't yet been proposed banning us from staying in the same country at the same time. (Not to give those worthless traitors at the UN any ideas.)

To the warrior, G. Gordon Liddy, who gets younger with each passing year, and to his Canadian producer Franklin Raff— looking forward to many more Mideast adventures together.

Thanks a million to Michael Reagan for all the segments and for continuing the legacy for all of us.

To the light in a dark world, Michael Savage—don't ever stop doing what you're doing. Thanks for the Jerusalem report segments.

To Tovia Singer—Our Thursday night broadcast has become an essential part of my life.

Thank you, Zelda Young, for giving me the opportunity to expand my audience to Canada on your great show.

INTRODUCTION

O NCE ISLAM DOMINATES AMERICA, anyone living inside must abide by our rules. There is no choice. You don't like it? Too bad. Go somewhere else and go to hell."

"If I saw you during the time of my [suicide] operation, I would not hesitate to blow you up."

"The Jews are corrupting humanity on earth. They are the source of all the problems in the world, and yes, they should be removed."

These are just some of the things Islamic terrorists—usually well-armed terrorists—said while I interviewed them in their strongholds.

When I was growing up, an Orthodox Jewish boy in Philadelphia, the last thing I thought I'd do for a living was schmooze with terrorists. I saw myself becoming a nice Jewish doctor—not a reporter who travels into war zones to interview anti-Semitic terror leaders. But sometimes life throws us curveballs.

I first became familiar with the name Osama bin Laden in the summer of 1998 after the terror chieftain issued a worldwide call for Muslims to kill American civilians and soldiers. His al-Qaida global *jihad* group then bombed United States embassies in East Africa, killing hundreds of people.

At the time, I was a biology student at Yeshiva University in New York City. I didn't really care much for international affairs. Like most other college kids my age, I grew up during a period of seeming calm and major economic growth for our country. War was something we studied in history class. The Middle East was a dysfunctional region that made the news every once in a while but didn't really affect our lives. The threat of terrorism, the prospect of an attack on American soil, was the furthest thing from my mind.

But there was something in bin Laden's *fatwa* against Jews and Crusaders that caught my attention and prompted me to take a second glance at the state of things. The rise of al-Qaida with attacks on tourists and U.S. troops in Somalia and the 1993 car bombing of our World Trade Center; the growing militancy of Islamist organizations, including those operating on U.S. soil and in Europe; the extremism brewing in Gulf states like Saudi Arabia; the very clear emboldening of terror-supporting dictators like Saddam Hussein and Yasser Arafat all pointed in one direction— a coming major conflict with militant Islam.

I researched bin Laden and terrorism on the Internet. I read books about *jihad*. I talked to some Mideast experts. But I felt those sources were missing something. Terrorism was mostly portrayed as a regional issue, a tool used by "militants" to gain specific political or ideological ends. I thought there was more. Something told me Islamic terror wasn't just about pieces of territory or getting U.S. troops out of the Middle East.

At the age of nineteen, I thought I'd investigate things for myself. I traveled to London and spent a weekend with the leadership of an Islamic extremist organization there called Al Muhajiroun that supported the goals of al-Qaida and held rallies in Britain calling for the downfall of America, Israel, and the U.K. and for the establishment of an Islamic regime.

Identifying myself as a Yeshiva student, I met with Sheikh Omar Bakri Muhammad, the leader of Al Muhajiroun, who later fled Britain. He told me all Muslims must work to "establish an Islamic state anywhere in the world, even in Britain [or America]."

I asked Muhammad about al-Qaida's operations. He explained attacks against U.S. interests had nothing to do with local politics. He said Islam was on the rise and America and its allies represented Satan on Earth. Muhammad informed me the Quran dictates the universe must be ruled by Allah's laws and that a worldwide Muslim *caliphate* would soon be created.

Muhammad explained Muslims were being called to join the *jihad* to bring down the West and spread Islam. He said men who died carrying out "resistance operations" against the U.S. and its allies would be sent by Allah to paradise. I penned an article on the interview experience, entitled "My Weekend with the Enemy," which was published in a few major newspapers, including the *Boston Globe* and *Jerusalem Post*.

I was surprised Muhammad agreed to meet me. My friends and family were shocked I would dare sit down with him. We are polar opposites. Muhammad's a *jihad*-urging *sheikh*. I was a Talmud-studying modern Orthodox Jew. I attended Jewish religious schooling my entire life from nursery school through college. I came from a tight-knit Orthodox Jewish community. I didn't even have a single non-Jewish friend until I moved to New York for university.

I returned from interviewing Muhammad a changed person. One conversation with an extremist *sheikh* taught me more about terrorism than all the Internet searches I could conduct. I was shocked by Muhammad's statements about Islam gearing up for war to destroy the West. This was not the picture presented by the news media, which failed to tell the larger story and many times seemed to almost justify terror.

Then came the September 11 terror attacks. Muhammad's statements and bin Laden's threats clearly weren't empty rhetoric. The war against our values became all too real. I quickly decided against medical school and went into Mideast journalism instead. After college I moved to Jerusalem and started reporting from there. I spent time with and interviewed Mideast terror groups on a regular basis.

I noticed upon speaking with terrorists that sometimes they tell it like it is. Still, sometimes they lie, and these lies need to be pointed out.

But you need to hear what the terrorists have to say. In the midst of America's war on terror, in the midst of our grand showdown with Islamofascism, with our boys and girls deployed in Iraq and Afghanistan and around the world to defend liberty, with Israelis dying in the Jewish state against the exact same enemy, it is crucial for all of us to understand the adversary we are up against. It is crucial for us to know how our enemy thinks and what they want to do with us. Even how your tax dollars—no, how *you*—fund terrorism.

Ever wonder what goes through the minds of terrorists when our mega-celebrities protest against the war in Iraq or against some of our anti-terror actions? Ever ask yourself who the terrorists want in high office, or how our nation's policies resonate with those seeking our destruction? Or what motivates a teenager or a grandmother or a professional to blow him- or herself up among a crowd of civilians? We'll schmooze with terrorists to answer these questions and many others.

I mostly interview Palestinian Arab terror groups openly allied with the global *jihad*. They say they see Israel as an outpost of America and for that reason the Jewish state has become the canary in the minefield in the war on terror. While some of the conversations presented in this book focus on terror against Israelis, the vast majority of the interviews are about the larger picture— the war against America.

Some people say it's controversial to interview evil, to dignify terrorists by talking with them. But from the way I see it, the problem isn't in talking with the enemy, it's with who's doing the interviewing.

My colleagues in the news media talk all the time to venom-spewing *jihadists*, to terrorist-sponsoring dictators and they ask softball questions and give terrorists a platform from which to spew their anti-American propaganda. These so-called reporters don't confront the terrorists with their lies; they don't give readers the proper context to understand things. Our reporters in the Mideast just take the terrorists' lying responses and go on to the next question.

The vast majority of the news media, the vast majority of reporters I work with here in the Middle East, are individuals who don't have the ability to tell good from evil. These reporters have absolutely no moral compass whatsoever. They think being a reporter means being "balanced;" they think it means one thing— that the truth is on both sides, that both sides are equal.

These reporters regularly refer to terrorists as "militants" with legitimate grievances. They go around presenting America's military campaign to eradicate terrorism as equivalent to attacks from terrorists. They think our anti-terror operations, which target terrorists who hide amongst women and children, which target *jihadists* launching rockets from civilian apartment buildings, which target gunmen who fire from a crowd of unarmed civilians, are morally equivalent to suicide bombers or terror leaders who fire rockets into population centers.

This is the lens through which most of our news is filtered today. This is the sick, twisted perspective of the so-called "balanced" reporters stationed with me, and it is these reporters who should not be interviewing terrorists.

In this book, you'll find no pandering to America's enemies. You'll find no excuses for terrorism. You'll find no rewording of the word "terrorist." As far as I'm concerned, if you're a member of a group that deliberately kills or threatens to kill civilians, you're a terrorist. If your organization sends suicide bombers into restaurants or nightclubs, you're a terrorist. If you call on teenagers to blow themselves up to achieve maximum casualties for the reward of eternal paradise with seventy-two dark-eyed virgins, you're a terrorist. If you fire rockets into cities to kill innocents, you're a terrorist. And if you harbor or support groups who seek to kill civilians, at the very least you're a terror supporter.

Why did the terrorists agree to talk with *me*? Why wasn't I killed or kidnapped?

I think a lot of Palestinian terror leaders I met were somewhat fascinated at the prospect of meeting a Jewish reporter. For many, I was the first Jew they'd ever knowingly interacted with. Some were stunned I'd debate them from a Jewish perspective. A lot of terrorists didn't know the kinds of questions I'd ask.

Some of these terrorists are interviewed regularly by other reporters. They are quite used to interacting with the media. Incredibly, some terror groups even have sizable "public relations departments" that are quite skilled at dealing with the news media.

But I believe the main motivation of the Palestinian terror groups in dealing with me is that they can claim to the English-language media they are not anti-Semitic. They can claim they are only fighting "occupiers" and not all Jews or Americans.

This, of course, is a big fat lie. They admit so in Arabic. These terror groups are at war with America, with Jews, and with Judeo-Christian values.

Still, the in-person interviews were quite dangerous. There were several times I thought I would not make it out alive. Other times I had some very entertaining experiences.

For me, though, the danger was worth it. I wrote this book ultimately because I believe America is in trouble. While we've made enormous advances in the war on terror the past few years, our great nation is encouraging terrorists to attack us and we don't even know it. That's right. Our actions, our media, our culture and our politicians are having a very deadly effect on the ground that could soon become disastrous.

Our response to terrorism since September 11 has been one of utter confusion and of mixed messages. Sometimes we take forceful action, sometimes we bend over backwards to accommodate the enemy and many times we think we can separate Islamic terrorism based on particular regions, as if terror in one part of the world is somehow different from terror elsewhere when the *jihadists* themselves admit they are fighting for the same cause.

We have failed to carry out a coherent policy against terror. We have failed to understand global terror and how to annihilate it. As a result, the terrorists are much stronger today than before September 11, when our war on terror began.

If the American approach to identifying, understanding, and dealing with terrorism is not reexamined in the very near future, if we don't immediately begin to understand how the terrorists think and respond to our policies, we face a devastating reality, with global *jihad* beating down our doorstep before we even realize what happened.

So brace yourself. You're about to take a trip into the viper's den of some of the most dangerous terrorist organizations in the world. And when you emerge from this journey, you might just see the world in a different way.

CHAPTER ONE

MADONNA, BRITNEY SPEARS STONED TO DEATH?

LIFE IF THE TERRORISTS WIN

"WE MUST NOT RECOGNIZE any government authority, or any authority at all besides Allah," said Faheed, a twenty-three-year-old student leader addressing about twenty Muslims gathered in the large classroom. I was the only non-Muslim in attendance.

Faheed's short beard complimented his brown turban, long white robe and a green military sweater with Arabic writing on it.

"We are Muslims," he shouted. "[The U.S.] is going to attack us! It is us versus them! Truth against falsehood! The colonizers and masters against the oppressed, and we will burn down the master's house!"

Continued Faheed to a supportive audience: "The U.S. is not strong. Vietnam, they lost. Somalia, they ran away from. America hasn't won anything since World War II. We can defeat America."

"Eventually there will be a Muslim in the White House dictating the laws of *shariah*!" he declared.

I didn't happen upon this speech during one of my visits to the terror-ridden West Bank or Gaza Strip. Faheed wasn't calling for the downfall of America from a classroom in Afghanistan or Iraq. This Muslim gathering wasn't taking place in France or Britain, which have well-known problems with Islamic extremists. Faheed was speaking in New York City. That's right. New York City.

It was March 2003. I was attending a closed (as in Muslim students only) meeting sponsored by the Muslim Student Association at Queensborough Community College in Queens, New York, just across the bridge from Manhattan, where I lived at the time. The MSA is an international organization of Muslim college students that boasts chapters in over a thousand colleges across America and Canada. It has been accused of promoting Islamic fundamentalism and inviting speakers who spew violent anti-American rhetoric.

I thought I'd check things out for myself. I had been fascinated with terrorism and with Muslims who live on American soil but seek the destruction of our values and institutions. Those in attendance at the New York speech likely thought I was a Muslim student, but no one asked. My Middle Eastern features allowed me to get away with that.

The event at Queensborough featured a lecture about Iraq by two American-based leaders of Al-Muhajiroun, a British Islamic fundamentalist organization that supports the ideology of Osama bin Laden, and whose worldwide leader, Sheikh Omar Bakri Muhammad, has long been suspected of ties with al-Qaida. In 2005, after Muhammad traveled abroad and was not allowed back to the U.K., Al-Muhajiroun's American branch changed its name to the "Islamic Thinkers Society."

Make no mistake about it. Islamists who want to replace our constitution with the Quran and who are urging on another September 11 live amongst us.

Another speaker at the MSA-sponsored event, Abu Yousuf, explained to me he speaks at many colleges throughout the New York area, and that most of his speeches are arranged by the MSA. In fact, Yousuf invited me to a speech he was giving the very next day petitioning for Islamic takeover; the speech was sponsored by the MSA at Marymount College in Manhattan.

There are other Muslim organizations and Islamic personalities in the U.S. that have petitioned for the replacement of the American government with an Islamic entity that would impose *shariah* law. In Europe, where the problem is more pronounced, Muslims make no bones about the way they want their societies run. In a poll conducted in September 2006 and broadcast on Britain's Channel 4 TV, 30 percent of the U.K.'s Muslims stated they would prefer to live under strict Islamic *sharia* law rather than be ruled by Britain's democratic system.

And of course we have the Middle East, where prominent terror groups like al-Qaida, the Muslim Brotherhood, and Hamas have declared war on everything our great country stands for. These groups want to impose their way of life on all of us. For them, Islam is on the rise just as it was during the days of Saladin, the Islamic conqueror. Terror leaders state openly they are fighting for one thing and one thing only—they want the world dominated by Muhammad's laws.

"Islam will enter every house and will spread over the entire world," said Hamas's Gaza leader and former foreign minister Mahmoud al-Zahar, at a March 2007 rally.

Actually, the terrorists told me they believe America is well on the road to becoming an Islamist entity.

"We see already in America a nucleus of Islam, a base for Islam. This will become bigger, stronger, more important, until Islam will take control and will seize the power in America and the world," said Sheik Saleh Faraj, one of the main leaders of the Islamic Liberation Party in the West Bank.

The Party, also known as Hizb ut-Tahrir al-Islami, acts in dozens of countries worldwide, including in Europe and Asia, to unite the entire *ummah*, or Islamic world community, into a single *caliphate* with the goal of Islamic domination of Planet Earth.

It took major convincing for Faraj to talk to me. He was sure I was a plotting Zionist agent sent to infect him with my venomous Judaism, but he finally agreed after a protracted argument with my translator, Ali.

Sheik Yasser Hamad, a cleric and a Hamas leader in the northern West Bank, told me he too sees Islam gaining a major foothold in America. He pointed to the ascension to power of Keith Ellison, who became the first Muslim elected to Congress when he won an open seat for Minnesota's Fifth Congressional

District in 2006. Ellison has many times publicly allowed his supporters to shout "*Allah Akbar*," or "Allah is great," and has confirmed to reporters that "in terms of my political agenda, my faith informs these things."

Hamad commented:

> In the West there is a huge spiritual emptiness and thirst for truth and it is not new that there is a growing phenomenon of thousands of people who convert to Islam.
>
> In the U.S., Keith Ellison, a Muslim, became governor and was sworn in using a Quran. This is proof of the spread of Islam and that Islam will one day dominate. We believe that this process will become bigger, stronger and larger.
>
> Prophet Mohammad, may Allah bless him, said that the sun will shine from the west. This will physically happen as part of the signs of Judgment Day and it will spiritually and practically happen as part of a big revival of Islam. Islam will grow in America and it may start its new campaign from the West.

Muhammad Abdel-El, a spokesman and leader for the Popular Resistance Committees terror group, affirmed, "America will be overthrown. We are seeing more and more signs that prove that the process had already started."

The Committees, one of the most active terror groups in the Gaza Strip, is responsible for scores of kidnappings, shootings, and rocket attacks, and was accused of bombing a U.S. convoy in Gaza in 2003, killing three American contractors.

Abdel-El pointed to the model of Europe, where he said Muslims are "taking over" without the need to resort to violence to acquire power. "In Europe there is no need for war because if people keep on joining Islam in these countries then Islam will become the majority, which I think is the process that is taking place now, so there will not be any necessity to have war with [non-Muslims]."

When Abdel-El said Muslims in Europe don't use violence to gain power he must have forgotten about mass Muslim protests in France and Britain that turned violent or the London transportation bombings in July 2005 and attempted bombings in June

2007, or the 2004 Madrid train bombings, among so many other examples of Muslims in Europe using violence.

◇

Conversations like these convinced me that the terrorists believe Islam will soon dominate America. But if Islam takes over, then what? What would life be like for Americans?

Faraj told me, "Your former defense minister, Donald Rumsfeld, once said that Islam doesn't allow and doesn't accept any partnership with any idea or principle about how life should be ruled and governed, and I must admit that he was right. This is the first and only time that I must admit that Rumsfeld was right. Islam cannot tolerate any idea or principle or any way of life that does not go with its laws and its vision and its rules."

Sheik Abu Saqer, a prominent Gaza-based preacher, a founder of the Sword of Islam terror group and a subscriber to the ideology of al-Qaida, explained if Islam controls the U.S., all American women, whether Muslim or not, must cover their hair.

"*Sharia* rules are clear, and according to these rules women need to be covered. This is the demand of our religion. Being and walking naked doesn't mean that you are enjoying more freedom; it means that you are going against Allah's laws and you are serving the enemies of Islam who want to empty our Islamic society from its values. Uncovered heads is a form of nudity."

Saqer is close to the Hamas and Islamic Jihad terror groups and is considered a *sharia* law expert. His Sword of Islam group has taken responsibility in Gaza for bombings of Internet cafes, pool halls, and secular music stores and is suspected of attacking a United Nations–funded school in Gaza accused of allowing girls and boys to play sports together.

Hamas's Sheik Hamad explained Islamic law enforcers would at first try to persuade American woman to cover their heads, but eventually females would be forced. Those women who refuse may be stoned.

"The women who will not cover themselves will be punished for not respecting the law. It could be jail. It could be stoning her.

5

It could be whipping her. It depends on the circumstances of the sin she made," Hamad said.

I expressed to Hamad my stance that forcing his beliefs on others is inhumane, but he objected:

"If you don't respect the local law in America, if you don't pay taxes, if you drive on a red light, aren't there sanctions used against you by your government? Of course there are and it's okay with you. Why is there a problem when it comes to the Islamic state that wants to impose its rules?"

The problem is that I'm not a Muslim and I wouldn't want to live a life dictated by *sharia*. Neither would my American female friends who don't want to cover their heads. America enforces a separation of church and state specifically to ensure against the imposition of religious ideologies and laws on those who don't subscribe. But the terrorists seeking to defeat our way of life have no problem forcing Islam down our throats.

"Once Islam dominates, anyone living inside the Islamic state must abide by our rules. There is no choice. You will abide or face the punishment," said Abdel-El.

Knowing full well he was talking to a Jew, Abdel-El said he would prefer that Jews vacate all lands taken over by Islam:

> I think there will no problem of Christians staying. Of course I do not mean those who were involved in killing Muslims in Iraq, Afghanistan and elsewhere. As for the Jews, for the safety of the state and I mean in the first place for the moral and social safety, and then the political safety, we prefer not to have them.

Abu Saqer agreed:

> As a principle we believe that Jews and Christians will always do everything in order to keep Muslims far from their religion. As long as they will not try to do so they can live in peace, but if they, especially the Jews, who are known for their bad character, will try to hurt Islam and Muslims, they will be treated harshly and may be killed.

I get frustrated and am pained by the terrorists' willful blindness every time a terrorist tells me Jews and Christians can live in peace in Muslim lands. Are they forgetting the Christians who live in so-called "peace" in the West Bank, Lebanon, Pakistan, Indonesia, or Kosovo, where they face regular Islamic persecution? Or all the Jews who lived under such "peaceful" circumstances in the Arab world they had to flee following widespread abuse after the establishment of the state of Israel?

◇

I personally experienced the warm hospitality of the Arab world toward Jews when I was banned from entering Syria because, according to officials from Syrian embassies on the U.S. and Jordan, I was Jewish.

I am an American citizen whose family has resided in the U.S. for many generations. In December 2005, I attended a well-planned trip to co-host the *John Batchelor Show*, a nationally broadcast radio program then syndicated by ABC Radio Networks. We wanted to broadcast for two days from Damascus.

Batchelor, producer Lee Mason, and I made arrangements with the Syrian embassy in the U.S. in advance of our trip. We were told by Ammar al-Arsan, the press *attaché* for the Syrian embassy in Washington, that the applications for all of our visas were approved, and that Damascus had sent an approval letter that would permit us to enter the country from Amman, Jordan. Syria's embassy in Washington was informed I am a Jerusalem-based American reporter; Syria doesn't allow entry to visitors with Israeli stamps on their passports, but the State Department issued me a second passport so that I could go on these kinds of trips. Jerusalem-based non-Jewish reporters have traveled to Syria.

But when we arrived in Amman, we were told by Eyad Alarfi, assistant to Syria's consul general in Amman, that visa approvals were granted for Batchelor and Mason, but not for me.

I spoke by phone to an official from the Ministry of Information in Damascus who declined to provide his name. At first he refused to suggest why I had been singled out and prevented from entering the country. Later in the conversation, however, he asked: "What religion are you?"

I refused to answer.

"You know what you are," said the official.

Mason, who made the initial arrangements for visas with Syrian media representative al-Arsan, said a red flag was immediately raised when my name was mentioned as one of the participants in the trip. He reportedly told her it would be better if I did not go. She asked if it was because I am Jewish. Al-Arsan replied: "Yes, it is." The third question on Syria's visa application asks for religion.

In protest of my denial, Batchelor and Mason refused their visas, and we broadcast instead from the terror-ridden Grand Hyatt Hotel in Amman. Leaders of the anti-Syrian government in Lebanon slammed Syria for not allowing me in. The droll, reliable Walid Jumblatt, largely considered one of the most prominent anti-Syrian Lebanese politicians, called Syria's refusing me "absolutely ridiculous. Syria is out of control. There is no reason in the world Klein should be denied entry into Syria. He should sue the Syrian government."

During our stay in Amman, we allowed Syria's ambassador to Washington, Imad Moustapha, to explain to our radio audience why I was rejected.

"We are a sovereign country and we have the right to decide who enters and who does not," was all Moustapha would offer.

He refused to answer the one question I had for him: "Will you issue me a journalist visa to enter Syria?" Moustapha attempted to change the subject, but I persisted.

When Moustapha still refused to answer, Batchelor interrupted, "Mr. Ambassador, will you issue a journalist visa to Aaron Klein, yes or no?"

Moustapha's "That's not the question" drew a sharp response from Batchelor who told Moustapha he took his refusal as a no and terminated the call.

Speaking to reporters about my visa denial, Batchelor said, "It seems like its 1938 and Czechoslovakia all over again."

> Aaron told me to go on to Syria and broadcast. But I told him that if I was to leave him behind, the enemy has won a victory. What we represent to the people of Jordan and Syria is that we don't separate people on the basis of race, color or creed.

In the end, after they were thoroughly exposed, Syria quietly apologized to me and offered to grant me a visa. Syrian officials even went out of their way to grant me a few interviews.

But don't be fooled by the Syrians or the conversations I had with terrorists. Just because they talked to me doesn't mean they like Jews. Palestinian leaders and terrorists regularly claim during English-language interviews they have no problem with Jews; it's only "Israeli occupiers" they despise, they say. What better way to drive home that lie than to treat an Orthodox Jewish reporter like royalty? But their deep-rooted anti-Semitism came up time and again.

◇

Jews and Christians who are not actually thrown out if Islam takes over America must live as second-class citizens. According to *sharia* law, non-Muslims are considered inferior; they cannot own land; no new synagogues or churches can be built in the Islamic state. Existing houses of worship may remain, but services cannot be conducted loudly or in any public fashion. The ringing of church bells or blowing of the ceremonial Jewish *shofar* are forbidden. Muslims are told to respect other religion's pre-existing holy sites, but for all those who want to know just how well Islam treats the holy sites it takes over check out the next chapter.

Non-Muslims living in the Islamic *caliph* are referred to as *dhimmis*, or protected persons. Defenders of Islam as a liberal religion claim since *dhimmis* are protected therefore Islam treats non-Muslims well. But think about it. The very use of the word *dhimmi* implies non-Muslims must be protected from something, and that non-Muslims are of such a different status they require protection. But protection from whom? The general population. The Muslims.

To merit "protected status," non-Muslims must pay special taxes, including higher commercial and travel taxes, and special taxes for the right to cultivate (but not own) land. All non-Muslims must pay the special poll-tax, or *jizya,* which basically is the non-Muslim's payment for his right to exist. The *jizya* is assessed at three rates according to the economic conditions of all males above the ages of puberty. Reminiscent of the yellow stars

Jews had to wear in Nazi Germany, several times in history non-Muslims living in the Islamic state had to wear at all times a special necklace that proved they paid their *jizya* taxes. Some Islamic scholars and clerics insisted the *jizya* be paid at a public ceremony that would include the humiliating act of striking the non-Muslim on the head or neck.

Think this *jizya* stuff is outdated? Think again. The few Jews who remain in Yemen must pay the *jizya* and other special taxes for protection. And they still are harassed. The Yemeni Jews fled their villages several times, such as in January 2007, after receiving death threats from local Islamic groups accusing the country's tiny Jewish community of serving as agents for "global Zionism."

When it comes to the legal system, in practicality Muslims take prominence over non-Muslims. A Christian or Jew cannot testify against a Muslim. Punishment for crimes committed by a Muslim against non-Muslims can be reduced; while crimes committed by a non-Muslim are judged harshly.

Sharia law is very clear about crime and punishment. "For every sin and crime there is a sanction," explained Hamad. "Prostitution: one hundred whippings; if the prostitute was married, he or she will be stoned until death; for a thief, his hand will be cut. But before enjoying the primitive nature of Islam and before you express how much you are shocked by our rules, I must say that these are not immediate sanctions, but they are used only if the person was warned."

Hamad explained prostitution doesn't mean selling sex; he said the Islamic definition applies the term to all extramarital sexual relations. But he boasted Islam's allowing men to marry many women was a perfect remedy for prostitution.

"In order to prevent prostitution and before reaching the sanctions of stoning or whipping, we will marry all our unmarried young. By the way, Islam allows the man to marry four women, so if he or she keeps practicing sex outside marriage and prostitution, in this case the sanctions mentioned in Quran will be used."

While men can marry many women, in Islam, women do not have the right to divorce their husbands. Only men can divorce. And they can do so very casually.

These stonings for "prostitution" are still carried out today in the Arab world.

In Iran, in 2004, a woman was buried to her chest and stoned to death after being convicted of committing adultery. Hajieh Esmailvand was found guilty by the Iranian authorities of having extramarital sex with her seventeen-year-old co-defendant.

The Iranian law regarding the matter is very specific. Article 102 of the Iranian Penal Code states that men accused of prostitution are to be buried to the waist and women to the breast in order to be executed by stoning.

Article 104 states that the stones should "not be large enough to kill the person by one or two strikes, nor should they be so small that they could not be defined as stones."

<>

All terrorists interviewed for this book agreed homosexuality will not be tolerated, either, if Islam dominates the U.S. Nasser Abu Aziz, the northern West Bank deputy commander for the Al Aqsa Martyrs Brigades terror group, said, "These sick people [homosexuals] will be treated in a very tough way. According to the law and according to the tradition they will not be allowed to practice their sexual deviation. If they insist, besides jail and legal punishment I think that the population will not tolerate this and may hurt these sick people.

"I want to tell those who will read your book, you may say I am primitive; well I say we prefer to be considered by you as primitives while we prevent social and physical diseases like homosexuality."

The Committee's Abdel-El said homosexuality was causing the moral collapse of the U.S. He blamed the allowance of gays in the military for America's losses in the war on terror.

"Because of these homosexuals in the military, you are now losing the war in Iraq, in Afghanistan. Israel your ally is withdrawing and will keep doing so from our lands...It is only a question of time before your empire will collapse because of homosexuality."

Abu Oudai, the Al Aqsa Martyrs Brigades's now-deceased rocket chief in the West Bank, told me Israel lost its war against the

Lebanese Hezbollah militia in the summer of 2006 because "the Israeli army is full of gays." Oudai, who I interviewed frequently, many times live on national U.S. radio, was killed by Israel during an anti-terror operation prior to the publication of this book.

Abu Abdullah, a senior leader of Hamas's so-called military wing, told me homosexuality would be "dealt with in an uncompromising manner."

I hope liberals understand what Abu Abdullah is saying. Do those who lobby for dialogue with our enemy or the creation of a Palestinian state not know what they are urging on? Do they think an Islamist society will tolerate liberal ideals? Try attempting a gay pride parade down the streets of Khan Yunis or Sadr City and see what happens. In fact, I can tell you what will happen since I asked the terrorists: the parade participants will be stoned.

"Of course homosexual parades will not be allowed," said Sheikh Saqer. "Now if homosexuals will ask for forgiveness once we take over and will follow Allah's laws and the rules of the Islamic state, they can live in peace in the Islamic state. If they will keep going against human nature like Allah fixed and designed, if they try a parade, they will be sanctioned according to *sharia* laws. Yes, they may be sentenced to death."

◇

All these Islamic rules would add stress to any ordinary American's life. Makes you want to go out and down a few beers. But don't even think about drinking. American bars and clubs will be shut down under *sharia*, say the terrorists. Alcohol will be strictly prohibited.

"Of course bars and clubs will not be allowed and will be shut down. Everything that goes against Islam and morality as Islam sees it will not be allowed," said Hamas's Abu Abdullah.

"You don't like it? Too bad. Go somewhere else and go to hell," he said.

And forget about American television, popular music, and movies; only Islamic culture will be tolerated.

"American culture is very cheap and very corrupting. Your American culture is based on capitalism, on democracy, sex, and other principles that go against the nature of human beings as Allah created. We will fight all that this culture represents and promotes," said Faraj.

"Only moral and respectful music and movies are allowed, and anything that doesn't suit our vision and our religion will be banned, even by force," Islamic Liberation Party leader Faraj said.

Defending Islamic laws, Hamas chief in Gaza al-Zahar told me, "I hardly understand the point of view of the West concerning these issues. The West brought all this freedom to its people but it is that freedom that has brought about the death of morality in the West. It's what led to phenomena like homosexuality, homelessness and AIDS."

Saqer said American culture is "empty of values. This is a culture that encourages deviations like homosexuality. Your kids want to be compared with the personalities they see on the movies, and so the value of men in the American culture is worth nothing. In your movies killing of human beings is something ordinary and natural. You even encourage this and incite people to be criminals."

I guess Saqer thinks the Palestinian media, which encourages suicide bombings and shows images almost daily glorifying death and *jihad*, is a glowing beacon of morality in broadcasting.

What about freedom of the press in the new American Islamic state? None of that will be had. The terrorists said once Islam rules us, American media outlets that don't conform to disseminating Islamic messages will be closed. They said the *NY Times*, CNN, the *Washington Post* would all be banned.

"The media will be closed not because there will be no freedom but because what is the logic of allowing the activity of media that can endanger the political and social stability of our state?" said the Brigades's Nasser Abu Aziz.

The terrorists took particular offense at the FOX News Channel, which some called a "network of evil."

Abu Abdullah said, "The evil FOX encourages a lack of respect to Islam and resistance movements and will cause moral confusion and negative political influence."

There is also a possibility music may be altogether banned if Islam takes over. Saqer explained some Islamic experts and sages, including those of the school of Egyptian scholar Sheik Yusuf al-Qaradawi, allow music; whole others, like those belonging to the Islamic Salafite school, forbid music.

"Regarding music, once we take over we will let the *sharia* council take its decision and I think it will try to reach a compromise between the different schools and visions," Saqer said.

I tried asking the terrorists what they thought of specific American cultural icons and personalities like Tom Cruise, Bob Dylan, Marilyn Monroe, even Hugh Hefner, but most weren't familiar with any of them. I asked about different American classic movies, like the *Wizard of Oz* or *Psycho*, but they never heard of those, either. With the exception of some celebrities who involve themselves in Mideast causes, the terrorists were largely clueless about our cultural personalities. There were only two U.S. celebrities I asked about that all the terrorists were familiar with: Madonna and Britney Spears.

"Unfortunately, I heard the names of Madonna and Spears on [Arab] television when parents complain that their children neglect their studies and their values because they are influenced by your cheap American music that you call culture," said Saqer.

All the terrorists called Madonna and Spears "prostitutes." (One called Spears a "fat cheap prostitute.")

I asked them what they would do with these two "prostitutes" if Islam took over America.

Al Aqsa's Nasser Abu Aziz said, "We will prevent your prostitutes from appearing on our TV. This is against all morals and not only against Islam. We will not allow our youth to be exposed to this pornography."

Saqer said Madonna and Spears would be asked to convert to Islam.

Hamas's Abu Abdullah told me, "At the beginning, we will try to convince Madonna and Britney Spears to follow Allah's way. But I honestly don't think they will follow. If they persist with their whoring music, we will prevent them by force. I don't think that I can be in the same place with these singers. They might be killed if they do not respect our laws."

MADONNA, BRITNEY SPEARS STONED TO DEATH?

The Committee's Abdel-El, whose group previously bombed Americans, said, "Their music video clips will be forbidden and these whores Madonna and Spears will be thrown in jail until they admit they made sins and return to the moral way. If they don't, they will be stoned to death or eighty times hit with a belt."

Abdel-El said even before Islam takes over America, he would personally kill Madonna and Spears if he ran into them. "If I meet these whores I will have the honor—I repeat, I will have the honor—to be the first one to cut the heads of Madonna and Britney Spears."

CHAPTER TWO

BIBLE USED AS TOILET PAPER?

WHEN TERRORISTS MEET HOLY SITES

"Islam has the highest respect for all monotheistic religions and peoples of faith."

Taysir Tamimi, Chief Palestinian Justice

"Our hands are outstretched and our religion calls for peace, not for war...for knowing each other and not for disavowing each other."

Sheikh Yusuf al-Qaradawi, Qatari Muslim Cleric and head of the Islamic Scholars Association

"In social terms, the pillars of Islam prescribe humility, teach tolerance, and respect diversity."

King Abdullah II of Saudi Arabia

"Islam is a religion that respects all the Messengers of God."

Dr. Mohamed Sayed Tantawi, Grand Sheikh of Al-Azhar mosque in Cairo

FOR AMJAD SABARRA, a Christian Arab pastor fortunate enough to serve in the world's oldest parish, October 2, 2002, started off just like any other normal Tuesday would on a fairly cloudless spring morning in Bethlehem. Sabarra attended his early duties, but said he was a bit surprised when ten armed Palestinian gunmen wandered into his sacred church, the Basilica of the Nativity of Jesus Christ.

"I approached the [gunmen] and explained that we do not allow arms in the Basilica and that they would have to leave. They did so quietly and politely. We then bolted the front door of the church," stated Sabarra in a recorded account.

Sabarra went about the rest of his daily routine, as did thirty other friars, four Catholic nuns, nine Greek Orthodox monks and five Armenian monks. What none of them could have known was that the gunmen who entered the Bethlehem structure that morning feared a pending Israeli anti-terror operation and were scouting the city for a safe haven; or that in about six hours, the clergy of the site believed to be the birthplace of Jesus would find themselves hostages in a real-life drama that would unfold on television screens worldwide and would see one of the holiest sites in Christianity thoroughly desecrated.

"About the conditions in which we left the church, it is true there was a lot of dirt," admitted terrorist Jihad Jaara five years later, speaking to me from exile in Ireland. Jaara, who was the Bethlehem-based chief of PLO dictator Yasser Arafat's Al Aqsa Martyrs Brigades terror group, was one of the main terror leaders of the fiasco that would become known as the siege of the Church of the Nativity.

<>

They say March comes in like a lion and goes out like a lamb. But for the Holy Land, March 2002 proved to be a lion-only month, marking one of the bloodiest thirty-one-day periods in recent Israeli history.

The month's first Palestinian terror bombing occurred on Shabbat afternoon March 2 in the Jerusalem neighborhood of Beit Yisroel, where a terrorist sent by the Al Aqsa Martyrs Brigades, the "military wing" of Arafat's Fatah organization, detonated his explosive belt amongst a crowd of Orthodox Jewish women waiting with their baby strollers for their husbands to return from prayer. The blast killed ten civilians, including an infant and her six-year-old brother; a mother and her three-year-old son; a twelve-year-old boy and four other adults. Another fifty people were wounded, many seriously. One later died of her wounds.

The month continued with terror attacks virtually every day, including suicide bombings against buses, shopping centers, and restaurants and deadly shootings against random passenger cars.

One notorious attack that month was a Hamas suicide bombing of a cafe across the street from then–Prime Minister Ariel Sharon's official Jerusalem residence. The blast killed eleven civilians, ten of whom were in their mid-twenties and were getting a quick bite to eat after partying. Fifty others were injured, including many who to this day suffer severe effects from the bombing. I would later live on the same street as the cafe bombing when I moved to Israel as a reporter in February 2004. On my way to work each day I would pass a plaque outside the cafe bearing the names of the victims, reminding me daily of terror's consequences.

In another infamous attack from March 2002, a Hamas bomber exploded himself on March 27 in the dining hall of a hotel in the northern Israeli coastal city of Netanya during the height of the Passover holiday. Twenty-two Jews eating their festive Passover meals were killed and nearly two hundred more were moderately to seriously injured by the blast on one of Judaism's holiest days.

The month went out roaring when a suicide bomber on March 31 struck a diner in the northern Israeli coastal city of Haifa, killing fourteen and injuring over forty civilians. In all, ninety-three Israelis were killed in Palestinian terror attacks that March, and at least 509 were wounded.

March was the height of over two years of continuous Palestinian terror following the collapse of U.S.-mediated peace talks between Arafat, Prime Minister Ehud Barak, and President Bill Clinton. Arafat walked away from negotiations in July 2000 at Camp David during which Barak offered the Palestinians a state in the Gaza Strip, West Bank, and eastern Jerusalem. Instead, the PLO leader returned to his fiefdom in Ramallah and started a terror campaign, termed the second *intifada*, aimed at pressuring Israel and "liberating" Palestine through violence.

Arafat's terror war galvanized the Israeli street and helped elect to office Ariel Sharon, who was perceived as hawkish and won by a landslide on a campaign against withdrawing from territory. (Of course, Sharon would later defy his own platform and unilaterally retreat under fire from Gaza.)

It was against this bloody backdrop that Israel decided to launch a major anti-terror campaign in April 2002, dubbed Operation Defensive Shield, which, Sharon explained, sought to "crush the Palestinian terror infrastructure in all its components."

Bethlehem, once a peaceful Christian town, had since the launch of Arafat's *intifada* become a hornet's nest of terror, housing an important infrastructure of the Palestinian militant apparatus. Many Christians earlier started emigrating from the city, eventually leaving behind a Muslim majority. Some of the Palestinian shooting attacks perpetuated during the bloody month of March 2002 were carried out by Bethlehem-area terrorists. The city's leadership of Hamas, Islamic Jihad, and Arafat's Al Aqsa Brigades was accused by Israel of planning multiple suicide bombings and other attacks.

As part of Defensive Shield, Israeli Defense Forces tanks, on April 1, 2002, surrounded Bethlehem and raided the ancient city the next day on a mission to arrest hundreds of terrorists.

Israeli troops entered in force on April 2. Heavy fighting immediately broke out on Manger Square, a major pedestrian district near the Church of Nativity. Overwhelmed by the large numbers of Israeli forces, roughly two hundred Palestinians, including a large contingent of terrorists—some very senior—fled the square and stormed the Church.

At about 3 p.m. the Church of Nativity's Father Sabarra reports he heard gunfire and shouting "in and near the Basilica." Upon entering the church, the good father said he and other clergy found "several hundred Palestinians running into the nave of the Basilica with several dozen men carrying guns and semi-automatics. Apparently, they had broken the front door of the church." The door had been bolted shut earlier that morning, after gunmen scouted the site.

Due to the church's sacred status and Israel's general hesitance to fight near holy sites of any faith, the Palestinian terrorists and gunmen who stormed the church likely assumed Israel would not continue fighting. In fact Jihad Jaara, one of the main terror leaders of the siege told me as much.

"We sought refuge in the church thinking this is a place for peace and where Jesus was born. It's very important to the world. It's a place we knew would be protected," Jaara said.

Jaara was high up on Israel's most wanted list. The terror leader personally carried out scores of shooting attacks, including the shooting of a public bus near Bethlehem that killed one Israeli man and crippled a woman. He's accused of planning suicide bombings and admitted to me he dispatched a bomber to Jerusalem's largest shopping mall, which is located just a few miles from Bethlehem. That bomber detonated his explosives prematurely. According to Israeli security officials, Jaara was an important link between Palestinian terror groups and the Iranian- and Syrian-backed Hezbollah militia in Lebanon.

I was a bit surprised that Jaara conceded he and his terror gang ran into the Nativity Church because they knew Israel respects holy sites and wouldn't attack them inside one of Christianity's most important churches. But he denied Palestinian gunmen scoped out the church earlier in the day as a possible refuge.

Incredibly, Ayman Abu Eita, who during the church siege was chief of the Al Aqsa Martyrs Brigades terrorist group in the Bethlehem satellite town of Beit Sahour, admitted to me that prior to Israel's raid, Arafat's Palestinian Authority directed Bethlehem-area terrorists to use the Nativity Church as a sanctuary and draw Israel into fighting there.

"The conspiracy was to make a siege and put all the fighters inside the church so Israel would make the siege. People from the Palestinian Authority collaborated with this conspiracy," said Eita.

I interviewed Eita in Bethlehem. He's also one of the main Fatah representatives in Beit Sahour. Eita is a Christian member of the Al Aqsa Brigades terror group. There are scores of Christians in Palestinian terror groups, but they are mostly Christians by consequence of birth only. These Christian terrorists are not religious. They do not accept Jesus as their "Lord and Savior." Many even grew up attending Muslim schools.

Eita said unlike most of the other "fighters" in and near Bethlehem, he didn't run into the church because he "understood the conspiracy."

"During the siege, I communicated with those inside and told them not to give the Israelis a list of the fighters inside because then Israel would start looking for the fighters who were outside and I was one of them," Eita said.

He claimed the PA collaborated with Israel to have senior Bethlehem "fighters" run into one place—the church—so Israel can attack the terrorists all at once, which is a ridiculous assertion. Nonetheless, Eita told me there were orders from the PA for the terrorists to seek sanctuary in the Nativity Church. This is a phenomenal admission. Israel was widely condemned for encircling the church after the terrorists ran inside. (The IDF could not just let the Palestinians escape; inside the church were thirteen of some of the most important terrorists in West Bank, plus dozens of other terror operatives and about fifty Palestinian "security officers" who also serve in terror groups.) But during our interview Eita dropped the bombshell that the church siege was orchestrated by the Palestinians.

◇

Upon entering Bethlehem and finding the terrorists holed up in the church, Israel immediately surrounded the holy site and attempted to starve the gunmen out while refusing to storm the structure for over one month. Trapped inside with the gunmen and Palestinian operatives were reportedly about forty-five unarmed Palestinians who ran in with the terror crowd and forty-nine church clergy.

On the second day of the siege episode, the Palestinians in the church refused to lay down their weapons, come out, and face arrest. Instead, according to insider accounts, terror leaders, including Jaara, began eating up food supplies and drinking beer and wine in spite of an Islamic ban on alcohol. Clergy trapped inside later told reporters top Palestinian gunmen slept on comfortable beds in an elegant apartment inside the church, using high-quality woolen blankets, while the civilians slept on cold tile floors in the main church downstairs.

Israel cut electricity to the area two days into the siege, the same day the church's unarmed bell ringer ran outside toward Israeli forces and did not obey orders to halt. Thinking the man was a suicide bomber, the IDF opened fire and killed the bell ringer.

Several days later, the holed-up Palestinian terrorists attacked the IDF from their positions inside the church. Israel secured the release of four clergymen and offered the gunmen inside the opportunity to either face trial in the Jewish state or be permanently expelled from Israel, but the gunmen refused.

"I would never accept Israeli jails; this means I would spend the rest of my life behind Jewish bars. I'd rather die," said Jaara. "About exile, we thought if we stayed in longer we could get better terms."

On April 23, three Armenian monks managed to flee the Nativity compound in coordination with the IDF. They immediately thanked the Israeli soldiers. One of the monks, Narkiss Korasian, told reporters the terrorists inside "stole everything, they opened the doors one by one and stole everything...they stole our gold, prayer books and four crosses...they didn't leave anything. Thank you [Israel] for your help, we will never forget it."

Later in the week, twenty-four Palestinians surrendered as part of a "food for people" deal forged between Israel and Arafat, but Israel decided against sending in the food, worried the provisions would draw out the siege.

On May 2, a mysterious fire broke out in the church early in the morning in the Greek Orthodox and Franciscan living quarter. Surveillance footage from an IDF blimp showed the church windows were blown outward by the heat of the fire, indicating the flames could not have been set by IDF forces, who would have broken the glass inward with firebombs, bullets, or flares. Many international news media outlets reported Israel started the fire in the important Christian church. Jaara also claimed to me the Israeli troops firebombed the church.

The siege finally ended March 10 when after thirty-nine days mediators agreed the thirteen senior terrorists inside, including Jaara, would be deported to European countries, twenty-six would be transported to the Gaza Strip, and the remaining gunmen would be allowed to go free.

After the fiasco, the church was found by reporters and Israeli forces to be in shambles. Four Greek monks told the *Washington Times* the Palestinian gunmen holed up with them seized church stockpiles of food and "ate like greedy monsters" until the food ran out, while the trapped civilians went hungry. The terrorists also were accused of guzzling beer, wine, and Johnny Walker scotch that they found in the priests' quarters. The monks said the indulgences lasted for about two weeks into the thirty-nine-day siege, until food ran out and those inside the church were forced to eat weeds and other improvised nourishments.

Perhaps one of the grimmest charges was made by Roman Catholic priests who told the *Times* some Bibles were torn up and used as toilet paper, and many valuable sacramental objects were removed.

"Palestinians took candelabra, icons, and anything that looked like gold," said Rev. Nicholas Marquez.

Immediately following the end to the siege, angry Orthodox priests showed reporters about twenty empty bottles of whiskey, champagne, vodka, cognac, and French wine.

"They should be ashamed of themselves. They acted like animals, like greedy monsters. Come, I will show you more," said one priest, who declined to give reporters his name. He reportedly gestured toward empty bottles of Israeli-brewed Maccabi beer and hundreds of cigarette butts strewn on the floor of the Christian holy site; he took the reporters to see computers taken apart and a television set dismantled for use as a hiding place for weapons.

"You can see what repayment we got for 'hosting' these so-called guests," said Archbishop Ironius, another cleric, as he showed reporters the main reception hall of the Greek Orthodox Monastery.

Ironius gave onlookers a tour of where the terrorists had broken in to the monks' quarters by smashing locked doors while, he said, the monks were praying downstairs.

Israel later claimed it found documents in the church implying the terrorists attempted to extort church officials for money in exchange for their assured safety.

There was enormous outcry in the Muslim world in May 2005 when an American magazine reported (but later retracted the story) that U.S. interrogators in Cuba flushed a Quran down the toilet. Hundreds of thousands of Muslims protested throughout the Middle East. And we all witnessed the deadly riots after a Danish cartoonist had the gall to depict the Prophet Muhammad. But according to the monks' accounts, Palestinian terrorists had no problem taking other religions' holy scriptures and using them for the vilest purposes imaginable. I confronted Jaara directly about the report he and his terrorist comrades used the Bible as toilet paper.

"I am not ready to hear your dirty accusations," he responded. "It is completely untrue that we used the Bible as toilet paper. We believe in the Bible and cannot do such a thing. On the contrary, the priests and monks had allowed us to pray our Muslim prayers, which meant Muslims praying in this very holy site to the Christians. This proves that the relations inside the church between us and those responsible in the church were excellent."

I laughed at Jaara's suggestion that priests and monks allowing dangerous, well-armed terrorists who were essentially holding them hostage to pray inside the Nativity somehow proved there were "excellent relations" with the church clergy. And I pressed again about the Bibles being used as toilet paper.

Jaara claimed the toilet paper account, told to reporters by priests, was really generated by Israeli intelligence agencies in an attempt to destroy the relationships between Christians and Muslims.

He went on to blame Israel for the siege and claimed it was the Jewish state that held civilians inside the church hostage for over a month.

This is a claim often repeated in many accounts of the church siege and it is patently absurd. Israel publicly tried during the entire ordeal to secure the safe passage of the clergy inside. It was the terrorists who refused to let out the civilians for fear once their human shield was lost Israel would storm the structure.

I asked Jaara whether the gunmen defiled the church in any way:

> No, not at all. We could not deface a place that is very holy to our Christian brothers toward whom we feel that we owe very much. How could we deface a holy place to the only community who helped us and who gave us a shelter while the Arab and Muslim countries neglected us and left us to our destiny in front of the Israeli army? During the thirty-nine days of the siege it was only the priests and the monks who helped and supported us.

I interjected: "But Jihad, the church siege took place in front of the world media. There is plenty of video footage of the condition the church was in when the ordeal finally ended. It was a big mess. The priests afterwards told reporters your group seized church stockpiles of food and 'ate like greedy monsters.' They say you gulped down alcohol. Israel says it found over forty explosive devices inside the church."

The terror leader conceded, "It is not a secret that inside the church there was a very serious lack of food. I don't remember that there were such problems as you describe. Still, we were 250 persons inside the church who suffered from the fact that the Israeli army prevented any food supply and we were obliged to eat the weeds of the gardens in the church. We did not blackmail the religious to give us their food. They kindly and with much generosity offered to share their food with us.

"As for the conditions in which we left the church, it is true there was a lot of dirt but it is normal to the conditions in which we were living. Thirty-nine days without any water and any possibility to move because of the snipers who were placed all around the church."

I asked Jaara what the church meant to him as a Muslim. He said it was an important site since Jesus "was a prophet for Islam.

Therefore we would not try to harm the church in any way." Many Muslims believe Biblical patriarchs and matriarchs, Moses, even Jesus, were prophets for Islam.

"We don't believe in all your versions of the Torah. Your Torah was falsified. The text as given to the Muslim prophet Moses [was different]. Abraham, Isaac, Jacob, Moses, and Jesus were prophets for the Israelites sent by Allah as to usher in Islam," Sheikh Taysir Tamimi, chief Palestinian Justice and one of the most prominent Muslim clerics in Israel, explained to me.

◇

Some terrorists holed inside the Church of the Nativity were Christian. I caught up in the Gaza Strip with Raed Shatara, a Christian member of Arafat's Fatah Tzanim militia who ran inside the Nativity church. He was exiled to Gaza as part of the deal that ended the church siege. Shatara is still active in the Al Aqsa Martyrs Brigades terror group. His brother was recently sentenced to sixteen years in Israeli jail for carrying out anti-Israel attacks.

Shatara claimed to me even though he drew Israel into battle at the church, he was a good Christian: "I am a Christian and I am proud to be Christian. Now saying this I want to add that Christians and Muslims, we are the same people, we are one big family."

I asked Shatara how as a Christian he can possibly justify bringing violence to the believed birthplace of Jesus.

"When the Israelis launched their operation and encircled Bethlehem we found ourselves having no choice, no other place to run away to but the church. We did not desecrate the church. You should understand that the Israelis were the ones who obliged us to find a shelter in the church."

Synagogues Now Rocket Firing Pads

The events in Bethlehem are just one of many high-profile occasions terrorists the past few years desecrated other religions' holy sites. One sickening desecration struck quite close to home for me.

A rabbi took my hand and gently nudged me to join the dancing. Men of all ages were swaying throughout the structure, singing "Am Yisroel Chai"—the Nation of Israel lives on—as they encircled a central platform from which the Torah is read to the congregation every Shabbat and on several weekday mornings.

The synagogue was filled to capacity. Males were dancing and singing on the main floor; women singing on upper level balconies. Some congregates were clapping and laughing, others broke down into tears, sobbing violently in each others arms. I joined in the chorus and the dance, quickly finding myself flooded with emotion like just about everybody else.

It was nearing midnight on August 16, 2005. The sound of rocket and mortar explosions could be heard sporadically throughout the night. I was in Neve Dekalim, the largest community of Gush Katif, the slate of Jewish towns located inside the Gaza Strip. In another nine hours, the residents of Neve Dekalim would be removed from their homes, some forcibly, and placed on buses that would take them into central Israel, never to return again to the Gaza Strip.

The Dekalim residents gathered in one of the city's two main synagogues to pray and sing together and to dedicate a new Torah scroll in honor of the town. Rabbis and local leaders delivered tear-ridden speeches promising the spirit of Gush Katif would live on forever and that the area would eventually be rebuilt. The dancing, the speeches, and the crying went on for several more hours that night. For many Dekalim residents I think it was the first collective outburst of mourning, the first communal realization that Gush Katif would indeed fall. For me it was the painful culmination of many eventful months spent with the residents of Jewish Gaza.

Starting April 2005, I rented an apartment in Ganei Tal, a beautiful, tree-lined neighborhood near Neve Dekalim in Gush Katif, months before the vast majority of the media arrived to report on Israel's historic Gaza evacuation. Most reporters showed up a few days before the withdrawal was carried out. For a good deal of them it very obviously the first time they had visited Gaza's Jewish communities, even for some journalists who had been reporting about those same communities for years.

I set up shop in Gush Katif and reported from there early on because for me the story of Israel's Gaza withdrawal was crucial. It was the litmus test for the concept of unilateral withdrawal, for the policy of retreat under fire. And trust me, the Gaza with-drawal was carried out under fire. The residents of Gush Katif and I endured months of heavy rocket and mortar barrages, with some of the deadly projectiles landing dangerously close to my apartment on many occasions.

I usually slept in Gush Katif two to three nights per week for the first few months I was stationed there. I lived in Gaza the entire month of August. During my stay there, I prayed in Neve Dekalim's main Ashkenazi synagogue many times. Ashkenazi congregations follow European Jewish customs as opposed to Sephardi, which maintains Middle Eastern Jewish tradition. I attended two bar mitz-vahs in the Ashkenazi synagogue, which also served for me on six occasions as a refuge from incoming mortar and rocket attacks. A large Sephardi synagogue was located nearby.

On August 17, 2005, Israeli security forces cleared out Neve Dekalim's residents. About three and a half weeks after that, on September 12, the last Israeli troop departed Gaza, officially marking Israel's complete evacuation of the territory. And then the Palestinians rushed in with pick axes and torches.

Immediately after the Israeli evacuation, Palestinians mobs de-stroyed most of the Gaza synagogues, including the Ashkenazi and Sephardi synagogues in Neve Dekalim. In front of international camera crews, young Palestinian men ripped off aluminum window frames and metal ceiling fixtures from the Neve Dekalim syna-gogues. Militants flew the Palestinian and Hamas flags from the structures before mobs burned the synagogues down completely.

It was one of the most brazen displays of savagery in recent memory.

Most homes in Gush Katif had been destroyed by Israel prior to the evacuation. I bore witness as some Katif residents, with tears streaming down their faces, set their own houses ablaze so the Palestinians wouldn't be able to utilize the structures for ter-ror. But the Israeli government decided to leave all of Gush Katif's twenty synagogues in tact.

Israel's Supreme Court had earlier ruled the Gaza syna-gogues should be bulldozed by the Israeli army, citing what is said was previous rampant Palestinian desecrations of other religions' holy sites as justification for the synagogue demolitions. But then–Prime Minister Sharon, who said he opposed the demolitions, put the decision to an Israeli cabinet vote. The cabinet decided against destroying the structures.

Israel's chief rabbinate had petitioned the Supreme Court to halt the synagogue destructions, arguing the demolitions contravene Jewish law.

Rabbi Shear-Yashuv Cohen, a member of the chief rabbinate, explained to me at the time: "According to Jewish law, synagogues cannot be destroyed unless new ones are already built, and even then, the issues are complicated. Here, the former Gaza residents don't have homes yet to live in, new synagogues have not been built, so there isn't even a question."

The Rabbinate also expressed fear Jews in other parts of the world may use the bulldozing of the Gaza synagogues as precedent to destroy other abandoned synagogues.

Two years later, in a complete turning of the tables, the area where the two main synagogues in Neve Dekalim once stood is used regularly by Palestinian terror groups as a military training zone and a site from which to launch rockets into Jewish cities bordering Gaza, according to terror leaders and Palestinian Authority sources.

A PA military post under the banner of "Guards of the Released Settlements" was erected at the entrance to Neve Dekalim, but none of the city's ruins have been rebuilt by the Palestinians as of this writing. There are plans for a Hamas-led university in Dekalim, but as of 2007 the area is being used simply to attack Israel. PA sources and terror leaders in Gaza tell me Neve Dekalim was used in 2006 and 2007 periodically as training grounds for their groups.

"We are proud to turn these lands, especially these parts that were for long time the symbol of occupation and injustice, like the synagogue, into a military base and source of fire against the Zionists and the Zionist entity," said Muhammad Abdul-El, a spokesman and leader for the Hamas-allied Popular Resistance Committees terrorist organization.

"The liberated lands of the destroyed ugly and Nazi settlements [Gush Katif] is our property, and we have the right to do whatever we feel is suitable for the struggle against the occupation and for the general interest of the Palestinian people," the Committees spokesman told me.

The Committees is a coalition of terrorist organizations operating in the Gaza Strip and the West Bank responsible for launching hundreds of rockets from Gaza aimed at nearby Jewish towns. The Committees' rocket attacks have devastated Israeli population centers nearby, including Sderot, a bustling city of twenty-five thousand and the port city of Ashkelon, home to strategic industrial facilities and one of Israel's largest electricity generators.

Incredibly, Abdel-El blamed the Palestinian desecration of the Gaza synagogues on the Jewish state, claiming the decision to leave the structures in tact was part of an Israeli conspiracy.

"The Zionists left these so-called synagogues in order to make that one day reporters like Aaron Klein would raise the pathetic and rude argument about what we have done to the poor Zionists' holy places. [Israel] left the synagogues behind so the world would see the Palestinians destroying them," Abdel-El said.

There you have it. The Palestinians are not to blame for acting like animals and burning down holy Jewish sites; instead the synagogue desecrations were Israel's fault and part of a vast Zionist plot to taint the Palestinian image.

Abdel-El was right in one sense, though. Israel should have known what the Palestinians would do once they got their grimy hands on the synagogues. There was no question the structures would be desecrated. Even Palestinian leaders admitted as much, showing just how much faith they have in their own society.

Prior to Israel's Gaza withdrawal, while the debate regarding the fate of the synagogues was still raging, Chief Palestinian Negotiator Saeb Erekat told me he begged Israel to destroy the structures. He too accused Israel of trying to make the Palestinians look bad.

"We of course have the highest respect for Judaism and the Jewish religion, but we cannot guarantee the synagogues won't be desecrated," said Erekat, speaking by cell phone from Gaza

City in September 2005. "We are very upset at Israel about this decision to throw their problems on us by leaving the synagogues. They are trying to make us look like barbarians and now we're stuck in a situation about whether to protect. We're damned if we do and damned if we don't."

Trying to make us look like barbarians? Mr. Erekat, the Palestinian mob that destroyed the Gaza synagogues are the worst kind of barbarians humanity has to offer.

According to Abdel-El, whose clan dominates large swaths of Gaza, the mob destruction of the synagogues was not planned but was a spontaneous outburst of "happiness" by young Palestinian men and children:

> The looting and burning of the synagogues was a great joy. There was no intention to desecrate them but this was part of the great joy the young men had when they destroyed everything that could remind us of the occupation. I want to say that all photos and video prove that those who destroyed or burnt were children and young people. It was in an unplanned expression of happiness that these synagogues were destroyed.

When I heard that I couldn't contain my anger.

"As a Jew and as someone who prayed in the Gaza synagogues I was horrified by what I saw when the Palestinians destroyed the holy sites. You should be absolutely ashamed of Palestinian society and ashamed of yourself for calling the burnings an expression of joy," I heatedly told Abdel-El. The terror spokesman shot back:

> I cannot believe how much guts and arrogance you have to accuse us of destroying and not respecting religion and the holy sites of others. You, would you call your son Muhammad? I am sure not. We the Muslims give our children the names of Moses and Jesus and Mary and this small example is enough to prove we respect the religions of others and shows who are the racists who express their hostility to Allah's religion.

Is Abdel-El kidding? The only reason some Muslims name their sons Moses or Jesus is because their religion claims these figures were prophets who foreshadowed Islam. They're not honoring Judaism by naming a son Moses—they're honoring Islam.

Abdel-El went on to accuse Judaism of disrespecting other religions' sites. He charged Israel turned "hundreds" of mosques into houses of prostitution and bars, a claim that has no foundation in reality.

"No nation in the world like the Jews has aggressed, destroyed, and desecrated the holy sites of other religions," he said.

I asked Abdel-El what a synagogue meant to him. He replied it's a symbol that represents a "divine religion that falsified the Torah."

"The Torah is not the same one that Allah gave to Moses. But although the Jewish Torah was falsified we respect all places that belong to the different religions."

Joseph, My Heart Weeps for Thee

> And Moses took the bones of Joseph with him: for he had straitly sworn the children of Israel, saying, God will surely visit you; and ye shall carry up my bones away hence with you.
>
> Exodus 13:19
>
> And the bones of Joseph, which the children of Israel brought up out of Egypt, buried they in Shechem, in a parcel of ground which Jacob bought from sons of Hamor the father of Shechem for an hundred pieces of silver: and it became the inheritance of the children of Joseph.
>
> Joshua 24:32

In one of the most flagrant, vile desecrations of holy sites in the history of humankind, on October 7, 2000, after Israeli troops retreated from a post just outside the northern West Bank city of Nablus following coordinated, deadly attacks against Jews there, scores of Palestinians stormed Joseph's Tomb and nearly destroyed the site believed to be the burial place of the biblical patriarch Joseph—the son of Jacob who was sold by his brothers into slavery and later became the viceroy of Egypt. Joseph's Tomb is the third holiest site in Judaism after the Temple Mount and the Tomb of the Patriarchs.

Within hours of the Israeli evacuation, smoke was seen billowing from the hollowed tomb as a crowd of Palestinians burned Jewish prayer books and other holy objects. Rioters used pickaxes, hammers, and later bulldozers to tear apart large swaths of the tomb structure and a beautiful *yeshiva* erected at the site. The dome of the Jewish tomb was painted green, and a mosque was subsequently erected in its place.

Seven years later, I caught up with the terrorist directors of the tomb desecration. The leader of the main group responsible told me the Israeli retreat from Joseph's Tomb "proves that when we are determined and when we apply military pressure against the enemy our attacks will work and bring about the defeat of [Israel]." More from him shortly.

<>

Joseph's Tomb is located outside the modern day city of Nablus. The vicinity of the tomb is widely acknowledged by historians and archeologists to be the important biblical city of Shechem, where Abraham built an altar to God upon his migration to Canaan and Jacob purchased a plot of land at which his son Joseph was later buried.

The Torah describes how Jacob purchased the land plot in Shechem, which was given as inheritance to his sons and was used to reinter Joseph, whose bones were taken out of Egypt during the Jewish exodus. Joseph's sons, Ephraim and Manasseh, are also said to be buried at the site.

Joseph's Tomb has never undergone modern archeological excavation, so some Western archeologists say the site cannot be proven authentic. But to me and to most Jews and to anyone regarding the site through a Biblical and historical perspective, the tomb is absolutely one of Judaism's holiest sites.

Joseph's life story is one of the most complete and instructive narratives of any personality in the Torah. The eleventh son of Jacob and son of matriarch Rachel, Joseph was thrown into a pit and then sold into slavery by his brothers, who were jealous that Joseph was Jacob's favorite son.

After he was falsely accused of trying to commit adultery with his master's wife, Joseph found himself in an Egyptian prison, where he made a name for himself as a talented interpreter of dreams. Among his fans was a temporarily imprisoned cupbearer for the Egyptian Pharaoh. The Torah relates the story of how Pharaoh once had a strange dream he needed help understanding and the cupbearer remembered Joseph, recommending the prisoner's services to the Egyptian ruler.

Joseph correctly interpreted Pharaoh's dream about seven fat cows and seven gaunt cows as meaning Egypt would have seven years of plenty and seven years of famine; he advised Pharaoh to immediately appoint someone to oversee the storage of vast quantities of food to survive the famine.

Pleased with Joseph's interpretation, Pharaoh made Joseph viceroy over the land of Egypt. Seven years of bounty were indeed followed by the famine Joseph had predicted and which Egypt overcame due to Joseph's rule. Joseph was eventually reunited with his brothers and father and maintained his Egyptian leadership position until he died an old man.

Shortly before his death, Joseph asked the Israelites to vow they would resettle his bones in the land of Canaan—biblical Israel. As detailed in the Torah, that oath was fulfilled when Joseph's remains were taken by the Jews from Egypt and reburied at the plot of land Jacob had earlier purchased in Shechem, which is believed to be the site of the tomb.

Yehuda Leibman, who until the Israeli retreat from Joseph's tomb in 2000 was director of a *yeshiva* constructed at tomb, explained, "The sages tell us that there are three places which the world cannot claim were stolen by the Jewish people: the Temple Mount, the Cave of the Patriarchs, and Joseph's Tomb."

Israel first gained control of Nablus and the neighboring site of Joseph's Tomb in the 1967 Six Day War. The 1993 Oslo Accords signed by Arafat and Prime Minister Yizhack Rabin called for the area surrounding the tomb site to be placed under Palestinian jurisdiction but allowed for continued Jewish visits to the Tomb and the construction of an Israeli military outpost alongside the holy site to ensure secure access to the Tomb for *yeshiva* students and for Jewish and Christian worshipers.

Leibman's *yeshiva*, the Od Yosef Chai School (which is Hebrew for "Joseph lives on"), was built at the tomb in the mid-1980s and housed volumes of holy books and a Torah scroll. *Yeshiva* students would arrive at the Tomb as early as six in the morning and would study there most days until midnight. They continued learning at the school daily even after the tomb area was transferred to Palestinian control. The tomb's Israeli military outpost protected the students.

There is data suggesting for more than a thousand years Jews of various origins worshipped at Joseph's Tomb. The Samaritans, a local tribe that follows a religion based on the Torah, say they trace their lineage back to Joseph himself and that they worshipped at the tomb site for more than seventeen hundred years.

But as they do with many important sites of other religions, the Palestinians claim Joseph's tomb is not a Jewish holy site at all but a Muslim one. Muslims say an important Islamic cleric who died about 250 years ago named Joseph Al-Dwaik is buried there and that the tomb is named after him. They claim biblical Joseph, who they say was not a Jew but a prophet for Islam, is buried at the Tomb of the Patriarchs in the ancient West Bank city of Hebron. (Muslims also call the Tomb of the Patriarchs, Judaism's second holiest site, a Muslim holy site that has no connection to the Jewish people.)

Following the transfer of control of Nablus and the general area encompassing the tomb to the Palestinians in the early 1990s, there were a series of orchestrated outbreaks of violence in which Arab rioters and gunmen attempted to force Israel to retreat entirely by removing its lone military outpost from the tomb, thus forcing an end to Jewish worship at the site.

Six Israeli soldiers were killed and many others, including *yeshiva* students, were wounded in September 1996, when Palestinian rioters and gunmen attempted to overtake the tomb, reportedly with the help of Palestinian police.

Eyewitness Hillel Leiberman, who studied at the Tomb's *yeshiva*, recounted:

After a large demonstration in the central square of Nablus, Arabs began to march on Joseph's Tomb. Within minutes, the tomb was surrounded on all sides by thousands of Arabs, who began to pelt the compound with rocks and firebombs. In addition, the same Arab policemen who regularly served on the joint patrol with the Israelis now began firing at the Israeli soldiers with their Kalashnikov machine guns.

Israeli soldiers [who were called as reinforcements] retreated into the thick-walled building which encompasses Joseph's tomb, and the Arabs advanced into the yeshiva [which neighbors the tomb], after setting fire to an army post and caravan which housed the Israeli soldiers. At this point, the Israeli soldiers again radioed for help.

The Arabs, upon entering the yeshiva, engaged in a pogrom reminiscent of scenes from Kristallnacht, when synagogues in Germany were ransacked by Nazis prior to the Holocaust. Sacred texts [in the *yeshiva*] were burned by Palestinians or torn to shreds, talises (Jewish prayer shawls) and sacred tefillin (phylacteries) were thrown to the ground, and anything of value was pillaged. The *yeshiva's* office equipment, refrigerators and freezers, beds, tables, and chairs, and all the food, were stolen.

The library was set afire, the structure of the *yeshiva* building was extensively damaged, and everything in it was in ruins. The only exception was the building of Joseph's Tomb itself, where the Israeli soldiers had taken cover, and the yeshiva's Torah scrolls, which the Israeli soldiers miraculously managed to save in the course of the riots.

Eventually, the Israeli soldiers gained control of the tomb. But the 1996 riots whetted the Palestinian appetite and served as prelude for what would come next. Israel failed to arrest or take any action against the perpetrators of the deadly riots, even though the leadership of the unrest, many of whom I later interviewed, was well known to the Jewish state.

Then-Palestinian leader Arafat painted the Joseph's Tomb riots as a victory for his people and a first step toward the eventual destruction of Israel. Arafat escalated tension on the Palestinian street as a way of pressuring the Israelis to retreat from more territory.

Official Palestinian media and West Bank mosques ramped-up rhetoric concerning the "liberation" of Islamic holy sites and regular land. Sites like Joseph's Tomb, which previously held no great value in Islam whatsoever, were suddenly positioned by the Palestinian propaganda machine as stepping stones along the greater path toward the "liberation" of the Al Aqsa Mosque in Jerusalem and the rest of the "Muslim lands of Palestine."

The Palestinians continued to attack Joseph's Tomb with regular orchestrated shootings and the lobbing of firebombs and Molotov cocktails. Security for Jews at the site increasingly became more difficult to maintain. Rumors circulated in 2000 that Prime Minister Ehud Barak would evacuate the Israeli military outpost and give the tomb to Arafat as a "peacemaking gesture." The Israeli army started denying Jewish visits to the tomb on certain days due to prospects of Arab violence.

Arafat returned from U.S.-mediated peace negotiations at Camp David in September 2000 and started his terror *infitada.*

Then the Palestinians went for the kill regarding Joseph's Tomb during the period of one bloody week in October and the cowardly Israeli prime minister caved in.

On October 1, 2000, Palestinian gunmen from Arafat's military wing, the Al Aqsa Martyrs Brigades terror organization, attacked Israeli border police at Joseph's Tomb. An Israeli policeman was shot by a Brigades gunman and bled to death after Palestinian forces refused to allow for his emergency medical evacuation.

Heavy fighting at the Tomb continued on October 2.

The next day, clashes led by the Al Aqsa Brigades injured an Israeli policeman and ten Palestinian rioters.

On October 4, Israeli Defense Forces Chief of Staff Shaul Mofaz sent troop reinforcements to the Tomb but noted he was empowered to withdraw the troops if the danger to them became "too high." Barak met with Arafat and U.S. Secretary of State Madeleine Albright in Paris to reach an agreement to end the Joseph's Tomb violence. A deal was concluded in which the Palestinians stated they will stop attacks and refrain from entering the Tomb; Israelis would pull back forces to pre-violence positions.

Rioting again erupted on October 5 after Palestinian clerics used the funeral of a Palestinian rioter who died of wounds sustained two days earlier to incite the masses. Gun battles raged at Joseph's Tomb between Palestinian gunmen and Israeli forces.

On October 6, Barak gave in to the Palestinian terror campaign and decided to completely evacuate the resting place of Joseph and give to the Palestinians sacred grounds promised in the Torah as an inheritance to the Jews.

An Israeli evacuation was undertaken the next day, beginning at 3:00 a.m., as soldiers clandestinely remove holy materials and a Torah scroll from the site of Joseph's Tomb. But Palestinian gunmen led by Arafat's Brigades terror squad fire at an Israeli convoy as it departed the Tomb, injuring one border policeman. The Israelis retreated completely.

Within less than an hour Palestinian rioters overtook Joseph's Tomb and began to ransack the site despite Muslim claims the Tomb is the burial place of an important Muslim cleric.

Palestinians hoisted a Muslim flag over the tomb. Amin Maqbul, an official from Arafat's office, visited the tomb to deliver a speech declaring, "Today was the first step to liberate Al Aqsa."

Palestinian mobs continued to ransack the Tomb, tearing apart books, destroying prayer stands, and grinding out stone carvings in the Tomb's interior.

One reporter described the scene: "The site was reduced to smoldering rubble—festooned with Palestinian and Islamic flags—by a cheering Arab crowd…"

On October 8 the bullet-riddled body of *yeshiva* student Lieberman, who penned the earlier eyewitness account, was found in a cave near the tomb. Leiberman, whose father was a professor at my *alma mater*, Yeshiva University in New York, had disappeared a few days earlier after he went to investigate reports of violence at Joseph's Tomb.

Palestinians on October 10 began construction of a mosque on the rubble of the Tomb and *yeshiva* compound. Workers painted the dome of the compound green, the color of Islam and thus became of Judaism's third holiest site.

◇

Through the Al Aqsa Martyrs Brigades terror group, I was put in touch with Abu Mujaheed, leader of the October 2000 attacks against Joseph's Tomb, and with Jamal Tarawi, who was the chief of a major cell of the Brigades in Nablus during the period of the riots. Tarawi, a nephew of Palestinian intelligence director Tafiq Tarawi, is a Palestinian parliament member who was arrested by Israel in May 2007.

The night before I was to meet in Abu Mujaheed near Nablus to discuss the tomb desecrations, I was overcome with some sort of forty-eight-hour stomach bug. The next day, October 11, 2006, I could barely get out of bed and had a high-grade fever. I had to postpone the terror meeting by a week. That same day, incredibly, an American student was kidnapped by Palestinian terrorists just outside Nablus in the very area and at about the same time I was to meet Abu Mujaheed. The student was held a few hours and was released unharmed. I couldn't help but think what could have happened had I showed up in Nablus that day. It was one of several close calls I would have while writing this book.

The next week I mustered the necessary courage—or stupidity—to meet with Abu Mujaheed, tomb desecrator. Mujaheed was charged by Arafat's Fatah militias with directing shooting attacks against the tomb starting in 1998 through the Israeli withdrawal in 2000. He described to me how the cells of his Brigades ambushed and attacked the tomb until the Israeli army ran away:

> We used to attack the tomb on an almost daily basis. Our fighters were divided into five to six cells. Each cell was composed of ten members and we used to crawl to the tomb and exchange fire with the soldiers. We led attacks in order to take away the Israeli flag. It was part of our resistance against the occupation. The goal was to chase the army of occupation from our land and the result [an Israeli retreat] proves that when we are determined we can defeat the Israeli enemy.

I agreed with Abu Mujaheed's analysis that the Israeli retreat from Joseph's Tomb absolutely proves Israel can be defeated. What other message can possibly be sent by Israel evacuating one of the holiest sites in Judaism in direct response to repeated Palestinian attacks?

I asked the terror leader, who is still active in the Al Aqsa Martyrs Brigades, how he can justify attacking Judaism's third holiest site.

With a straight face, he denied all reports, including from major media outlets and actual Israeli Defense Forces video footage, that his group shot at the Tomb site, claiming instead his attacks were directed only at the adjacent Israeli military outpost.

"The Israelis were the first in the world to turn a holy site into a military base, a very fortified military base. We never attack any holy place. Our religion forbids us to do so. We attacked the military post that the Israelis placed there. It is now a holy site. When the Israelis were here it was a military base," Abu Mujaheed said.

I explained to Abu Mujaheed that Israel stationed troops at the tomb specifically to protect worshipers from his terror group.

An official IDF statement put it best:

> The military compound set up next to the shrine was to safeguard and protect the site and the safety of worshippers, in accordance with the agreement with the Palestinian Authority. Claims by the Palestinians that the site was a military compound are blatant lies and possibly an attempt to legitimize the criminal and vulgar desecration of a Jewish holy site.

I also scoffed at Abu Mujaheed's absurd claim Palestinians never attack holy places.

"You don't attack holy sites? Explain to me the video footage of Palestinian rioters and gunmen burning down the Tomb's *yeshiva*, bulldozing parts of the holy tomb, and then painting its dome green," I said. "To me this it the most barbaric behavior imaginable," I continued. "Even animals don't behave like this."

That statement got the terrorist tomb desecrator upset and sent him on a verbal rampage in which he accused me of being the animal.

"You Jews are the animals who do not respect holy sites. We see how you don't allow people to pray in the [Temple Mount's] Al Aqsa mosque."

(I must stop him here and point out his deception. The only people who are restricted from praying on the Temple Mount, Judaism's holiest site, are Jews and Christians. We'll get into that in a later chapter.)

Continued the venting, anti-Jewish desecrater: "You are the animals who not only desecrated holy books and the holy Quran in prisons like many of our heroic prisoners witnessed...I even think that some Jewish settlers and Israeli Army officers are below the evolution of animals, they are insects or even less."

He went on to accuse Jews of falsifying the Torah and Jewish history to claim Biblical Joseph was a Jew when indeed he was a Muslim and that Joseph's Tomb houses a Jewish patriarch, when, he explained, the site actually entombs a Muslim *sheikh*.

I accused Abu Mujaheed's group of shooting at unarmed worshipers at the tomb, another well-documented charge, but he denied that, as well.

"We never shot prayers. We never shot innocents. It is possible that if a prayer was armed he was shot by us, but we never shot an unarmed prayer."

Mujaheed claimed he didn't know how *yeshiva* student Hillel Leiberman, whose shot-up dead body was found in a cave near the tomb, was killed. He absurdly suggested Leiberman was shot by Israel while trying to protect the tomb.

Tafiq Tarawi, who led a major cell of the Brigades responsible for many of the tomb attacks, also claimed to me the Palestinians didn't kill Leiberman.

"This is one more Israeli lie that the Palestinians had shot this guy. We respect all religions and we respect all prayers," said Tarawi. Since he is now a Palestinian lawmaker, Tarawi would not confirm to me whether he was directly involved in the tomb attacks during his tenure with the Al Aqsa Martyrs Brigades, during which he led a Brigades cell in the vicinity of the tomb.

I asked Tarawi what Joseph's Tomb means to him. He called it a "holy site where our fathers and grandfathers and all Muslims used to pray at the place of an old Muslim personality. This is part of our holy sites and part of our cult and faith and not the Jews."

Denying history tying Jews to the tomb for thousands of years, Tarawi said, "Only after the Israeli occupation (in 1967) we started to hear this version of the tomb being the tomb of Joseph from the Torah. This is one more Israeli lie."

Tarawi and Abu Mujaheed said they would never allow the Jews to again establish a *yeshiva* at Joseph's Tomb as long as it is under Palestinian control.

"A *yeshiva* is an institution," said Abu Mujaheed. "An institution can be the beginning of claiming rights and these claims can bring once again the Israeli army to establish a base in the place and we cannot accept this. If the Jews try to build a *yeshiva*, we will shoot at them."

As I stood there and stared in the eyes of these terrorist desecraters, these gunmen who led a campaign of violence against one of the most sacred sites in my religion, I found I was actually not angry with them. How can I blame terrorists who do not have an ounce of humanity or decency to them and who so wantonly disregard history and reality? I cannot fault evil for being evil. And I cannot be upset when their society, which preaches suicide terror and extreme anti-Semitic propaganda, desecrates holy Jewish sites the minute Israel evacuates.

No, instead I was furious at the Israeli government. How can Barak possibly charge Palestinian society with protecting Joseph's Tomb as a Jewish site when most Palestinians deny there is any Jewish connection to the structure? Did Israeli officials actually believe Arafat's Brigades gunmen, who led daily shooting campaigns against the sacred monument, would allow freedom of worship once the Israelis retreated?

And I was angered at the hypocrisy of the international community for its failure to hold the Palestinians to any standard of civilized society. Yes, there were some condemnations of the Tomb attacks from Washington and European capitals. But those condemnations were followed by world pressure applied against Israel to retreat from still more territory and more holy sites.

And I was fuming at my fellow Jews. Where were they when Joseph's Tomb was desecrated? Can you imagine the Muslim response if Israel bulldozed the Al Aqsa Mosque, Islam's so-called third holiest site, and converted it into a synagogue? The Muslims would unleash holy hell. They'd launch World War III. And yet when Judaism's third holiest site was so violently molested you didn't hear much from world Jewry. Sure, American Jewish organizations issued the traditional press releases expressing "shock" and "outrage" at the Joseph's tomb desecrations, but where were the mass protests? There was a tiny handful of Jews who acted, including the valiant Susan Roth, chairperson of the Eshet Chayil Foundation, which paid to have the few remaining holy objects from Joseph's Tomb transferred to Rachel's Tomb in Bethlehem, which is still safe...for now. But where were the calls from world Jewry for Israel to retake the site or at least for the Palestinians to respect it? Why are Jews still ignoring the issue while Joseph's Tomb is being held hostage?

I cannot speak for world Jewry but as a *bona fide* member of the tribe I can say American Jews are too consumed with maintaining their stock portfolios and vacation homes in Boca Raton to concern themselves with such trivial matters as the desecration and now utter neglect of Judaism's third holiest site.

Joseph, my heart weeps for thee.

CHAPTER THREE

HI, MY NAME IS AHMED, AND I WANT TO BE A SUICIDE BOMBER

B EFORE I DRIVE YOU TO HELL, enjoy your tea and our hospitality," said Ahmed, gazing dead straight into my eyes.

Ahmed is a twenty-two-year-old Palestinian student from the northern West Bank city of Jenin. He's about six feet tall, with an athletic build, short-cropped hair, and dark brown eyes. He says he is part of a "normal Palestinian family; we're not poor but far from being wealthy."

Ahmed hopes to complete his college studies in 2008 and says he has a good prospect to get married. He occasionally lifts weights, plays soccer with friends, and watches television, particularly news and historical programs. He spends some of his free time browsing the Internet.

From what I could garner, Ahmed and I have a few things in common. Both of us are religiously oriented. Like me he comes from a large family—Ahmed falls second in the line of four boys and three girls; I'm the oldest of ten children, four boys and six girls. He shares a room with two of his brothers and doesn't get much privacy. Before I went off to Yeshiva University in New York, I shared a room with two of my brothers. The only privacy I ever took in was when I went to the bathroom.

Ordinarily I could see myself hanging out with Ahmed. Maybe play some sports together. Go to a cafe. Listen to music. But Ahmed and I weren't engaging in friendly banter. In fact, I don't even know his real name; I was asked to just call him Ahmed, and halfway into our conversation, Ahmed said he wanted to kill me.

Our talk, conducted through the good graces of my translator, Ali, was being monitored and filtered by Abu Ayman, a scary-looking, dark-featured man in his late twenties, whose stern gaze stopped Ahmed several times from divulging too many personal details for fear I would expose him to the Israeli authorities.

Ahmed has been recruited by Islamic Jihad, an Iranian-backed Palestinian terror group, to become a suicide bomber. Abu Ayman was the commander of Islamic Jihad in Jenin.

Together with the Al Aqsa Martyrs Brigades, which is the declared military wing of the Palestinian Authority's Fatah party, Islamic Jihad is responsible for all of the suicide bombings in Israel in 2005, 2006, and 2007, including a bombing at a shwarma eatery in Tel Aviv in April 2006, which killed American teenager Daniel Wultz and eight Israelis.

Islamic Jihad is one of the most active terror organizations in the world when it comes to suicide attacks. The town of Jenin, the terror group's main stronghold, is sometimes called "City of Suicide Bombers" since the vast majority of Palestinian bombers originated in its narrow, densely populated enclaves. The place is a suicide bomber breeding zone.

According to Abu Ayman, Ahmed is a top recruit and has "great potential" to become one of the next suicide bombers to infiltrate into an Israeli city and blow himself up among civilians, perhaps in a restaurant or at a nightclub. Ayman personally recruited Ahmed after the twenty-two-year-old made it known to local terror leaders he wanted to become a suicide bomber.

"I pray that Allah gives me the honor to be dead in an operation. This is the supreme and the noblest way to ascend to Allah," Ahmed tells me.

Ayman sat with Ahmed, myself, and Ali in the dining room of a small, sparsely furnished apartment in the center of Jenin. A woman and four children were in a second room of the apartment. The children were playing loudly and occasionally peered into the dining room, looked at us, and started laughing.

The walls of the dining room were plastered with propaganda posters of Islamic Jihad leaders, including Ramadan Shallah, the terror group's supreme commander who lives in Damascus under Syrian protection. One particularly flashy poster featured the face of Mahmoud Tawalbeh, a local Islamic Jihad leader killed during an Israeli anti-terror raid in 2002. Tawalbeh was somewhat infamous in Palestinian terror circles because he sent his brother on a suicide bombing mission.

"The martyr Tawalbeh is an inspiration for what it means to sacrifice for Allah," said Ayman.

"Do you want some sugar?" Ayman asked, as he poured Arabic samovar tea into a small glass for me.

I don't know what it is, but terrorists always serve the best tea. I remember every terror interview I conduct by the taste of each cup of aromatic Arabic tea that was served. The tea helps calm my frazzled nerves during these unpredictable journeys. And arriving at this Jenin apartment was quite a nerve-wracking feat.

Driving from Tel Aviv, about twenty miles away, I was instructed by Ayman to park my car at the main Israeli checkpoint just outside the entrance to Jenin, a city entirely controlled by the multiple gangs and thugs that comprise the Palestinian Authority security forces. From the checkpoint, Ali and I were instructed to take a local Palestinian taxi into the center of Jenin, where we waited about ten minutes, likely to ensure we weren't being followed.

A white Ford Escort with no license plates raced up to us. We were told by two men armed with black American assault rifles to get in the back seat. We were driven through a narrow alley until we arrived at an apartment complex.

Ali and I exited the car. The armed men scanned the area and asked us to remove the batteries from our cell phones, a routine I was used to by now. The Israeli Defense Forces is known to use cell phone signals to track exact locations of wanted terrorists. Apparently, the IDF can even track a cell phone when the device is turned off, as long as the battery is still inside.

Ayman, who was high on Israel's most wanted list of terror-ists, greeted us at the door of the apartment, which he said did not belong to him. I am told Ayman left his shelter in another sec-tion of Jenin to meet us. The two armed men waited outside the apartment and stood guard. Sitting quietly inside the living room, his hands folded, was Ahmed.

Ahmed didn't seem to fit the profile of what many believe is the make-up of the average Palestinian suicide bomber. He's not poor. His situation is not desperate. He told me his life is not all-consumed by a hate for Israel. He seemed quite intelligent. I'd venture to guess he is actually content with his place in life. So why in the world would this guy sitting across from me want to blow himself into little bloody pieces while trying to murder and maim as many Jews as possible?

"I originally decided to become a martyr after I saw what the Israeli army did in the refugee camp of Jenin in the big military campaign of April 2002," begins Ahmed.

Ahmed was referring to an Israeli anti-terror raid in his hometown, in which Palestinian leaders accused the Jewish state of a "massacre," claiming the Israeli army had wantonly killed over five hundred Palestinian civilians, including many women and children.

Most international news media at first simply reported the Palestinian fabrications. But it was quickly determined that fifty-six Palestinians, mostly gunmen, were killed in the raid, which had been provoked by a series of deadly suicide attacks inside Israel reportedly planned and directed from the terror infrastruc-ture in Jenin. Twenty-three Israeli soldiers had also died in the Jenin battle, because IDF troops had conducted house-to-house searches expressly in order to minimize civilian casualties by avoiding air attacks.

Continued Ahmed, "My desire to be a [bomber] became stronger when I understood what status I will have in heaven if I sacrifice myself for Allah. Every time somebody else dies as a martyr in a bomb attack, I pray for him but I feel jealous. I want to be where he is now and I pray that Allah will one day offer me this occasion and this honor."

"Is your main motivation for becoming a bomber is to serve Allah?" I asked.

"Yes, of course. Allah gave Muslims the possibility to gain their prize and payment in different ways. There are those [Muslims] who pray and fast only and respect Allah's commandments, and there are those who wish a higher prize. And the highest prize is given to those who sacrifice themselves, their lives, their bodies and everything in this world."

What Ahmed said immediately struck me because it contradicted claims by some Western academics and many of my colleagues in the news media that Palestinians become suicide bombers because they are poor and angry at Israeli occupation.

Whenever there is a suicide bombing in Israel, much of the international news media race to find the bomber's family and produce so-called human interest stories painting the murdering terrorist as a victim of Israeli aggression driven to revenge. The stories are all pretty much the same for every suicide bomber.

Once, in February 2002, I was actually caught in a terror attack when I was visiting Israel as a student. A Palestinian terrorist opened fire on Jaffa Street, a busy shopping mecca in Jerusalem, killing two women and injuring thirty others, before police officers chased down the terrorist and shot him to death. Such shootings are considered suicide missions because, in Israel's extremely armed society, the terrorist has no chance of escaping alive.

Thankfully I was inside a store at the time of the attack, shopping for presents to bring home, but I heard the gunshots, which began about one hundred feet from where I was situated. I emerged when it was all over to bear witness to the deadly mess. Blood was spewed on the streets. The injured were screaming. The body of a dead woman was surrounded by onlookers.

And then I got back to my hotel room and turned on CNN. The gunman was labeled an "activist" from Islamic Jihad, and a story was broadcast against the backdrop of the Israeli army's killing of a Hamas "activist" two days earlier, as if there were some sort of moral equivalence between the two events.

A CNN correspondent was reminding her viewers of the "Israeli occupation, which creates despair in the territories that many say leads to such suicide attacks."

Never mind that there is no historic precedent for any Western nation to resort to terrorism in response to "foreign occupation," humiliation, or poor living conditions.

Even the French, who during Nazi occupation were living under far worse conditions than any current inhabitant of the West Bank or Gaza, never once resorted to terrorism. And the wives and children of German soldiers were exposed and could have been easily targeted.

I asked Abu Ahmed about CNN's claims that suicide bombers are motivated by despair. He balked, actually calling it "Israeli propaganda."

He explained Islam forbids suicide and that a "martyr" cannot act based on feelings of desperation. A suicide bomber, Ahmed said, is motivated by the "will to sacrifice myself for Allah."

Ahmed's recruiter, Ayman, chimed in, agreeing with Ahmed's assertion. Ayman said his Islamic Jihad terror group only accepts Palestinians who want to become martyrs for the sake of serving Allah.

"Part of my role is to decide who is really suitable and who is not. And this process demands basically to see who really wants to carry out the operation because he wants to reach Allah as a *shahid* [martyr] and who wants just to die, to kill himself, or in other words to commit suicide.

"In Islam suicide is forbidden; therefore, we never recruit somebody who just wants to kill himself because of the feeling of vengeance towards the Israelis or because he has psychological problems and the operation is a way for him to escape these problems. And we don't recruit people who don't know what they are doing," said Ayman.

And Ayman knows a thing or two about suicide bombings. At twenty-eight years old, Abu Ayman cut an impressive, muscular figure. He was about six feet with dark features and a military-style crew cut.

According to Israeli and Palestinian security officials and Islamic Jihad sources, Ayman was a central player in six suicide bombings carried out inside Israel since March 2005. Thirty-eight Israelis and two Americans were killed in the attacks. The terror leader had a more minor role in several of fourteen other suicide bombings perpetuated between December 2001 and 2005, killing ninety Israelis. Israeli officials say Ayman is one of the most important links between Islamic Jihad in the West Bank and the terror group's leadership in Syria. He was appointed overall commander of Islamic Jihad for the Jenin region in February 2007, after the former commander was arrested by Israel.

Ayman did not deny to me his involvement in planning the suicide bombings.

But he did lie when he claimed his terror group doesn't send Palestinians with psychological problems. Islamic Jihad has the past few years sent bombers with disabilities. Israel says it twice caught mentally retarded Palestinian teenagers attempting to infiltrate with suicide bomb belts.

But Ayman claimed these kinds of candidates "are never sent to the operation. Only those whom we feel are one hundred percent convicted and one hundred percent understand what it means to be a martyr and want to do so for religious motives, only those are sent to the operation."

Ahmed added, "The goal of becoming a *shahid* is that it is the way to reach Allah. The goal is satisfying Allah and his instructions. No money interests, nothing. No brainwash, no pressure." Strangely Ahmed claimed his goal is not even the killing of Jews.

"Did I hear you say your goal is not to kill Jews? Isn't that exactly what you will do as a suicide bomber?" I asked Ahmed.

"Maybe the fact that I was born in Palestine has sharpened my religious conscience, but I believe that even if I was in Chechnya, in Iraq, Afghanistan, or anywhere else I would want to be a martyr.

"It is Allah's satisfaction that is important to me no matter where I live. But as we live in this part of the world the way to reach Allah for me is through fighting the Zionist enemy. It is the jihad, the sacrificing that is important."

Now that we were on the subject of killing Jews, I became a bit nervous.

Okay, I was downright frightened. Here I was, an out and proud Jew in the middle of suicide bomb city talking with a potential bomber and a senior leader of a terror group sworn to the Jewish state's destruction.

I knew exactly what I was doing before I requested the interview, but there are always those moments when things suddenly become so much more real and you ask yourself, what did I get myself into and how I going to get out alive? But I tried my best to conceal my discomfort.

"These *clichés* about suicide bombings not being about killing Jews are impressive but I know you are aware that you are speaking to a Jew. Perhaps you are telling me what I want to hear. Tell me the truth. You want to kill Jews, don't you?" I asked. My heart started racing.

Ahmed replied, "We were never taught to hate Jews but to hate the occupation of the Zionists to our Islamic land that the Zionist entity with the conspiracy of the world has stolen and occupied. Jews can have their state but not on our lands and until this goal is achieved every Muslim must fight this entity.

"The Jews stole this holy Islamic land and we must fight them, but I am looking to receive what waits for me in the next world."

Of course, Ahmed was lying to me. He was absolutely taught to hate Jews. The Palestinian news media daily spew the most vicious, anti-Semitic propaganda imaginable. The official Palestinian school system teaches students Jews are descended from pigs and monkeys; that we are subhuman devils who drink the blood of Muslims and Christians and must be killed wherever we are found. But let's put that aside for now. It was time for the golden question.

"You talk about fighting them, the Jews. I'm an American Jew. Do you want to kill me?" I asked, biting back my words the moment I mustered them.

Ahmed started laughing. "You are here and nobody hurts you and nobody thinks to do so. But if, unfortunately for you, if you will be in a place where my [suicide] operation will take place, I will not feel sorrow," he said.

Then Ahmed turned serious. "You American Jews are fully partners with the Zionists and even more dangerous than the Israelis because of the international support you give to the Israelis in their massacres against our people and the maintenance of the occupation."

At this point I started nervously browsing the room to ensure Ayman wasn't reaching for a suicide belt to strap on to Ahmed to blow me up.

"So if after today's meeting you saw me in a cafe in Jerusalem that you were sent to attack, you'd still try to blow it up?" I asked.

"At the moment there will not be a place for feelings and hesitations. If I go in an operation it means that I decided to leave behind my loved ones—my mother, my father, brothers and sisters, all my family and my friends. And if I am capable of this I would not give you a break just because we met for one time. I will not hesitate to blow you up," said Ahmed

"Meanwhile and before I drive you to hell in an operation, enjoy your tea and our hospitality," he said.

It was then that it dawned on me that I was probably the first Jew that Ahmed had ever met. After the upbringing he had, I was surprised he didn't inquire as to what happened to my horns, or whether I had the features of a pig under my clothes.

The Quran actually states several times Allah turned Jews into pigs and monkeys.

Among several examples:

> So when they [the Jews] exceeded the limits of what they were prohibited, We said to them: 'Be you monkeys, despised and rejected.' (Sura 7:166)

> Those [Jews] who incurred the Curse of Allah and his Wrath, and those of whom he transformed into monkeys and swines. (Sura 5:60)

I asked Ahmed whether he believes Jews are descended from pigs and monkeys.

He replied, "I know where this question comes from. You think that we all are naïve or bad from birth or that we were exposed to brainwashing. We just follow what we are demanded in the Quran to do because if we do not do so we will be attacked, occupied, controlled, and killed by these enemies of Islam."

"You didn't answer my question," I persisted. "Do you believe I come from pigs and monkeys?"

"The Quran tells us that Allah was upset with the Jews because of their negative behavior towards Moses and Allah's commandments and Allah shouted to the Jews, 'Be pigs and monkeys.' I don't know if physically Allah turned them to pigs and monkeys, or it was a way to tell them that they are as terrible as pigs and monkeys. The most important thing is that this is what Allah, may he be blessed, thinks that the Jews deserve to be."

Ahmed called Jews the nation "known for killing Allah's prophets and the nation that in our days wants to control the world or at least this part of the world, from the Nile to the Euphrates.

"Meanwhile they [Jews] are controlling the U.S., its media, its financial system, and its administration," he said.

"Did We Find the Seventy-two Virgins Yet?"

One of my great fascinations with suicide bombers is their fervent belief that when they explode themselves they are greeted in heaven by seventy-two dark-eyed virgins. The concept of the virgins as reward is driven home regularly by Palestinian *imams*, the news media, and the school system. Even Palestinian pop culture: a music video airing in September 2006 on official PA television, for example, encourages viewers to "martyr" themselves in exchange for eternal paradise and seventy-two beautiful "maidens." The video depicts a man who dies in *jihad* and is immediately escorted to "heaven" where he is greeted with several white-robed women with flowing hair.

In a November 10, 2006, Palestinian television broadcast, Sheik Imad Homato, a prominent West Bank religious cleric, instructs Palestinians to strive for a violent death in which the martyred corpse has "no head, no legs, his body completely burned...intestines outside, fingers...gone."

Homato explains to his viewers that Allah blesses the "first blood" of the suicide bomber, who "sees his place in paradise, is shielded from the great shock, and marries seventy-two dark-eyed maidens."

I only wish I could be there to greet every Palestinian suicide bomber in the afterlife so I could see the look on his face when the little suicide bombing pawn first realizes he's been lied to; when he suddenly understands he will spend the rest of eternity in a fiery furnace watching endless *Golden Girls* reruns with the sound of a Mariah Carey CD buzzing in the background.

One of the greatest differences between Judaism and Islam is in the religions' priorities. Jews are taught to serve the Creator in this world to achieve heaven in the next, but also that all Jews merit a place in heaven. The main emphasis in Judaism is life, not death. Ninety-nine percent of the Torah deals with life and how to live it. The Torah only vaguely refers to heaven, with little description of what it is. All Jewish sages agree heaven is for the soul and encompasses spiritual, not physical bliss.

Islam focuses on the "world to come," and how to achieve paradise. The emphasis is on the afterlife. Paradise is mostly described as a physical world replete with the most baseline physical pleasures, including free sex and wine.

It's interesting because the Quran doesn't specifically state that good Muslims get seventy-two dark-eyed virgins each. The only reference to the seventy-two maidens are in a Quranic verse quoting Muhammad as being overheard saying, "The smallest reward for the people of paradise is an abode where there are eighty-thousand servants and seventy-two wives. Verily, for the *muttaqun* [righteous], there will be a [paradise]; gardens and grapeyards; and young full-breasted [mature] maidens of equal age; and a full cup [of wine]."

So Muhammad describes the whole of heaven for regular Muslims as consisting of seventy-two wives (not to mention alcohol, which is forbidden to Muslims in this world) but doesn't specify whether each individual Muslim gets his own abode or if there is just one abode with seventy-two wives. Nothing in the

Quran specifically states that the faithful are allotted seventy-two virgins apiece.

And the only reference to maidens in the Quran, when referring to the righteous, doesn't state anything about seventy-two. Just simply that paradise for the righteous has "gardens and grapeyards; and young full-breasted [mature] maidens of equal age; and a full cup [of wine]."

I always have fun with this when meeting my terror "friends." I ask them to show me where in the Quran it specifically states suicide bombers get seventy-two virgins. They usually struggle with the challenge for a few minutes and then change the subject.

Once, when interviewing the senior gun-toting leadership of the Al Aqsa Martyrs Brigades terror organization in the northern West Bank city of Nablus, the biblical Shechem, some pretty scary terrorists got a little testy over the subject.

Rusty Humphries, who is a nationally syndicated radio host with a nightly audience of millions of listeners, came along with me to Nablus and conducted much of the interview. Nablus is known as the stronghold of the Al Aqsa Martyrs Brigades and is entirely controlled by Brigades-affiliated militias.

The Brigades, together with Islamic Jihad, took credit for all suicide bombings in Israel from 2005 to 2007 and regularly carries out shootings and rocket attacks against Jews population centers.

Humphries, recording the interview for his show, pressed Ala Senakreh, the West Bank chief of the Brigades, on the issue of the seventy-two virgins. Senakreh, by the way, was wielding a massive machine gun he claimed to have used less than twenty-four hours earlier to shoot at Israeli soldiers. Senakreh is well known for his regular appearances on Palestinian television where he spews deadly threats against Israel.

Another important detail here is that in the room with us were nine other well-armed terrorists who basically comprise the top of Israel's most wanted list of Fatah terror leaders.

Humphries had several of the terrorists, including a man called Nasser Abu Aziz, flip through the Quran for about five minutes looking for the seventy-two virgins. Abu Aziz, the Brigades' deputy commander in the West Bank, had his hand in at least five suicide bombings in Israel and personally shot dozens of times at Jews living in the West Bank. At over six feet tall, wearing military boots, camouflage pants, and a thick black vest, and wielding a nice-sized pistol, Abu Aziz is by far the scariest looking terrorist I ever laid eyes on.

"Look up the seventy-two virgins in the Quran for me, because the Muslims in America say it is not true," prodded Humphries during the interview.

"Of course it is true! It is mentioned in the Quran. In your religion you have the book," retorted Ala Senakreh, the Martyrs' chieftain.

"I just want you to tell me chapter and verse where it is. And also many moderate Muslims, they call them moderate in America, believe that Islam is a religion of peace and that there should be no violence," said Humphries.

"There is not violence. This is *jihad* for God," Senakreh stated.

"Let's find the seventy-two virgins," Humphries persisted.

Senakreh and several others were flipping through the Quran but were not coming up with much. We engaged in general banter about Islam and the Israeli-Palestinian conflict, but Humphries kept insisting the terrorists find the Quranic verse promising seventy-two virgins to suicide bombers.

The frustrated Al Aqsa Martyrs Brigades terrorists tried in vain to change the subject several times but Humphries kept at it.

"Hey! Has anybody found the chapter and verse of the seventy-two virgins yet?" asked Humphries. The terrorists were becoming visibly agitated.

I tried to signal to Humphries to stop asking about the virgins. I shook my head at him and tried to steer the conversation in other directions. I generally don't think it's a good idea to piss off a bunch of terrorist killers while you are on their territory and they have enough ammunition to blow us all to Allah's Paradise. But clearly Humphries thought otherwise.

"Do we have the virgins?" Humphries asked.

There was Arabic mumbling amongst the terrorists, but still no answer. Nasser Abu Aziz shot angry glances at me.

I truly believed we weren't going to survive the interview. I pictured Humphries and me making Arab propaganda pronouncements on an al-Qaida-style video before our heads were chopped off by masked Ala Senakreh and Abu Aziz.

I actually started making deals with G-d about the improvements I'd make in my life if only He got us out of Nablus alive.

And Humphries asked again.

"You guys find the virgins?"

Finally, Abu Aziz stated, "The Quran says, 'Fight those who fight against you, and never be the one who aggresses.'"

"What verse is that?" asked Humphries.

"Verse 1-8-9," replied a proud Abu Aziz.

But Humphries blew the whistle.

"Okay, but still no virgins. Still looking for the seventy-two virgin thing, huh?" Humphries said.

After about five minutes of agitated conversation, Abu Aziz announced he found the Quranic verse promising seventy-two virgins.

"OK, we have seventy-two virgins in the Quran, let's pull it out. OK, we found the seventy-two virgins thing," said Humphries.

"This is Al Amran verse 1-6-8, which says that those who get killed in favor of God are not considered dead people [but are] alive people between God's hands."

"Where are the seventy-two virgins?" Humphries asked as my face turned white and my stomach nearly jumped out of my throat.

Disappointed, Ala Senakreh conceded to us, "The *virgins* are mentioned in the Quran but the experts [who] interpret it considered *seventy-two virgins*. Virgins are mentioned in the Quran but not the number of seventy-two."

At that point I stood up and announced to the room Humphries and I had an important dinner date and that we had to leave.

The terrorists escorted us to my car. I think they were as happy to see us go as I was relieved to still be breathing. On the phone later Ala Senakreh told me never to bring Humphries back to Nablus again.

<>

Now back in Jenin with a real live potential suicide bomber and his *jihad* recruiter, I thought I'd ever-so-slightly test fate again and ask Ahmed about the seventy-two virgins.

"Show me exactly where in the Quran it states you will get seventy-two dark-eyed virgins for blowing yourself up amongst civilians," I asked Ahmed. But he was smarter than our hosts in Nablus.

"You and I, we do not discuss Allah and the Quran. I will tell you more the moment that I will explode myself when there will be one dark-eyed virgin who will carry up my soul to the sky."

I figured I'd just let that one go. I had no intention of creating a Humphries-style game of chicken about virgins a second time around. I'd had my lifetime share of annoyed terrorists scouring the Quran for seventy-two virgins. I focused instead on the implications of a Muslim heaven filled with virgins.

"You talk about so-called martyrdom being divine. About being rewarded in the next world on supreme spiritual levels for what you say is a gift to Allah. And yet you tell me that what awaits you after a suicide operation is an eternity of sex with virgins. This is the most baseline physical pleasure imaginable. This is your religious version of heaven?" I asked.

"Let me explain something to you," said Ahmed, as he began a theological exposition:

> The world, the lower one we are in now, it is temporary. Allah examines the loyalty of human beings, asking you in this materialistic world to avoid all that is tempting, all that pleasures you on earth, and to dedicate yourself to Allah.
>
> This doesn't mean that Allah does not think it is good to take part in these needs of sex, in the pleasure of drinking alcohol, enjoying nature and other stuff. The point is that non-Muslims do those things in this world while ignoring Allah and all moral rules, while Muslims are asked to do a tremendous spiritual effort on earth in order to gain these other [physical] pleasures in the next world.
>
> I don't know how you Jews see these physical pleasures, especially after the Torah that Allah gave you was falsified, but in our religion all spiritual efforts are

asked from us on earth and it is much more difficult. So
it is not that all the story is about sex. You do free sex
now, I do not.

Ahmed then informed me I will go to hell for having free sex
and that he will go to heaven.

"In heaven I will do and will enjoy what you did during your
life in this world. The difference is that after these years you will
burn in hell forever and I will, after my years in this world of
faith, restraint and patience, enjoy Allah's pleasures forever."

An amazing juxtaposition: A want-to-be suicide bomber telling me I will go to hell.

"Do you really think you will go to heaven for killing innocent civilians during a suicide operation?" I asked.

"You are treating in a ridiculous way this issue, but this is in
the Quran. Go and, Allah forbid, ask Allah about this point. We are
promised in the Quran to have the dark-eyed virgins and that's it.
The Quran is full of verses glorifying the *shahid*, the martyr."

It Ain't Easy Being a Terrorist

Palestinian *sheikhs* and terror leaders have no problem sending
fanatic teenagers to their deaths, but they themselves hide behind
civilians, drive luxury cars, and live in beautiful apartments
while so many others reside in slums in the United Nations–
fostered refugee camps in the West Bank and Gaza Strip.

With few exceptions, every terror leader I interviewed for this
book was surrounded by women and children during the interview. They do this because they know the Israeli army won't intentionally attack a home filled with civilians.

Islamic Jihad's Abu Ayman, whose job is to send suicide
bombers into Israel, seemed to me the usual brand of civilian-
using terrorist. And I made no bones about bringing that up.

"It's pretty easy to send others into population centers to blow
themselves up, but if you think suicide bombings are so important
why don't you become a martyr yourself?" I asked him.

Expressionless, Ayman made some excuse about Allah choosing him to be a planner and recruiter and not a suicide bomber.

He said his role as a leader in the Islamic Jihad terror group exposes him to possible Israeli assassination and so by deduction he was as brave as a suicide bomber.

He then offered a ten-minute sob story about how being a Jihad leader isn't easy and requires much personal sacrifice. He claimed Ahmed's life as a potential bomber is much easier than his.

"To be a [potential] martyr in a bomb attack is an easier life than mine as a wanted man who sleeps every night in different places, many times in forests and caves far from my wife and children. This is much harder than the brother who explodes himself," Ayman said.

But for someone complaining he stayed "far" from women and children, it sure was strange we were conducting an interview in an apartment filled with women and children.

Ayman continued with a straight face: "Sometimes I think that I want to sleep in the arms of my wife. That I want to take my wife and little children on a trip, but I gave up all these things and devoted myself to Allah."

"You say you devote your life to your god. So what you're telling me is a life devoted to Allah means sending suicide bombers into Israel to kill civilians?" I asked.

Ayman explained that since Israeli military installations are too difficult to infiltrate for attacks, suicide bombers "therefore must go to any place where he can kill members of this enemy."

Ayman pronounced all Israelis are military targets.

"As long as Israelis do not react against their government and its policy, we will never consider them as innocent civilians and they will always be a legitimate goal for our attacks," said Ayman.

I asked Ayman how he goes about picking the lucky Palestinians who merit becoming Islamic Jihad suicide bombers. Ayman said he doesn't go out to cultivate or recruit potential attackers because there were more than enough volunteers. Rather, Ayman described his role more as approving applicants and providing the bomber with logistics and an explosive belt—a tool, Ayman said, that will "drive the martyr to heaven."

"Far from the negative image of someone like me as exploiting naïve characters and putting pressure on poor guys to go out and explode themselves, I am more of a technical facilitator for someone enthusiastic about becoming a martyr."

Ayman says his Islamic Jihad terror group only accepts Palestinians who want to become martyrs for the sake of serving Allah.

He said on the day of an attack he will accompany the potential bomber throughout the day "to ensure he does the proper preparations."

Many terror experts believe potential bombers are followed by terror leaders preceding an attack to ensure the bomber doesn't change his mind at the last minute.

Ayman said on the day of an attack, a suicide bomber must spend as much time as possible praying to Allah. The bomber must be "totally clean like it's his wedding day," Ayman said, explaining purity represents the "holiness" of the martyr's mission and his "marriage" to Allah. Contrary to multiple films on suicide bombers, Ayman said Palestinian bombers don't shave off their body hair.

After a suicide bombing, Islamic Jihad pays monthly stipends to the families of a "martyr," Ayman said.

"But the payments are not a salary or a price for what their son and daughter did, but as a way to thank the family and to diminish their financial suffering because many times the volunteer contributed to the finances of his family," Ayman clarified.

I talked with Ayman about the role of other countries like Iran and Syria in financing and directing Palestinian terror attacks.

The biggest Palestinian terror leaders don't live in the West Bank or Gaza. They reside in Syria and regularly travel to Iran. Islamic Jihad chief Ramadan Shallah operates openly from Syria, where he gives media interviews and makes public appearances. Hamas chieftain Khaled Meshaal also lives in Syria with frequent trips to Iran.

And what does Iran get in exchange for directing Palestinian terrorism? The ability to stage distractions and foment regional violence and instability any time it wants. Plus, controlling Palestinian terror keeps Iran a major Middle East player.

One leader for the Al Aqsa Martyrs Brigades who directs the group's rocket infrastructure in the northern Gaza Strip once openly admitted to me he fires rockets for whoever pays him, whether Iran or anyone else. I jokingly inquired how much it would cost for a few Qassam rockets lobbed at CNN's Gaza branch. He said $10,000.

Following a bombing that killed six Israelis in the costal town of Hadera in October 2005, Abu Carmel, a leader of the Al Aqsa Martyrs Brigades in Nablus, who acknowledged his group took part in the attack, told me the suicide bombing was directed from Damascus.

But during our in-person interview, Ayman denied that Palestinian terror groups are controlled by outside parties.

"This is one more nonsense that shows that there is no logic in what you are saying and that you enjoy repeating what the Israelis tell you," charged Ayman. "The fact is that we want to carry out attacks every day but the conditions on the ground make it difficult. When there is an occasion to carry out an attack we, we just carry out the attack."

"Our Human Bombs Are the Most Effective Weapon"

As an Orthodox Jew little gets to me more than when so-called religious leaders pervert their religion to exploit the devout into doing things they shouldn't be doing. This happens on a regular basis with all religions in all parts of the world. But nothing is more extreme or more evil than the Islamic *sheikhs* who preach terrorism and instruct their followers to commit suicide in order to kill others in the name of Allah.

Perhaps nowhere is support for terrorism more prevalent than in Jenin, where polls show its residents are proud most Palestinian suicide bombers originated in their town.

Sheikh Salem Abu Muumen, revered by potential bomber Ahmed, is considered one of the most important religious leaders in Jenin. He's a charismatic man with a well-composed demeanor and is known within West Bank Islamic society for his deep knowledge of *sharia* law.

According to Palestinian Authority security officials, Muumen is close to the radical wing of the Islamic Jihad terror organization. The PA officials and Islamic Jihad sources identify Muumen as an important religious figure in mentoring Jenin residents who wish to become suicide bombers. The sources say Muumen aids the young recruits in spiritual preparations necessary to engage in martyrdom, even instructing the bombers which Quranic verses to read before exploding themselves.

Muumen commands his followers to seek death through *jihad*. His speeches to his Jenin congregation claim the greatest fate of all is to die in a *jihad* operation against the Zionist enemy.

I debated Muumen Jew to fanatic Muslim liar. Without beating around the bush, I started off by aiming right for his jugular:

> Sheikh, I think you are perverting Islam and justifying suicide bombings because suicide attacks as a tactic works. Because suicide bombings are your way of bringing worldwide attention to the Palestinian cause. Because the Palestinians don't have a military so you fight by attacking civilians off guard. Because outside players like Iran and Syria use Palestinian terror for their own ends.
>
> And you're perhaps the most important player in all of it. It is you that instills these lies that suicide bombers go to paradise and get seventy-two virgins. You're the reason Palestinian teenagers think they are serving Allah by killing Israelis. What is your response if I say I think you are lying to teenagers and brainwashing them into believing they get paradise?

I think the *sheikh* did not expect an immediate punch, but he shot back without flinching, telling me I was in no position to criticize him.

"I am glad that you are showing a deep understanding of Islam and that you have the capacity to analyze Islam and to tell us what is Islam and what does it allow or forbid," he said sarcastically. "It is not bad for a young American Jew whom I doubt if you even understand everything about Judaism," he said.

Muumen agreed with my assessment that suicide attacks are used as a tool by Palestinians.

"Because of the gap between us and the enemy [Israel], and the lack of military and technology abilities, martyrdom operations are the tool that we adopted in order to reach a terror equilibrium with the enemy. It is obvious that our human bombs are the most effective weapon we own."

Like Ahmed and Ayman, Muumen denied suicide bombers were brainwashed, claiming the Quran guaranteed "the greatest prizes of all" to *shahids*:

> When you find it suitable you people say that we are primitives and when it is more suitable you turn us into devious and strong people who are masters in brainwashing. There is no brainwashing. It is the religious motivation in the Quran and the religious duty that encourages the great numbers of our people to be suicide bombers.

I asked the *sheikh* how he can support suicide bombings when the Quran condemns suicide.

Muumen seemed a bit taken aback when I started reading from verses of Muhammad's testimony:

> [2:195] You shall spend in the cause of GOD; do not throw yourselves with your own hands into destruction.
>
> [4:29, 30] O you who believe…You shall not kill yourselves. GOD is Merciful towards you. Anyone who commits these transgressions, maliciously and deliberately, we will condemn him to Hell. This is easy for GOD to do.

Smiling, perhaps pleased I brought the debate to his playing field—the pages of the Quran—the good *sheikh* offered me his interpretation of the verses I read forbidding suicide. And in his interpretation lies the problem.

"You are reading into the Quran all wrong," Sheikh Muumen charged. "The difference between suicide and being killed as a martyr in a suicide attack is huge. A person who commits suicide kills a soul, a spirit, a person and this is completely forbidden by Allah who creates us and has the right to decide when our life comes to its end.

"Killing yourself in suicide is a sin but killing yourself in suicide as part of suicide bombing attack against the enemy is not forbidden because in the attack you kill those who are considered by Islam the enemy of Allah and of Islam."

Muumen said the Quranic verse I quoted about not throwing yourself into destruction actually requires Muslims to become suicide bombers.

"You throw yourself in your own hands to destruction when you give up *jihad* and don't participate in a suicide bombing against Islam's enemies as part of *jihad*," the *sheikh* stated.

Muumen claimed he was backed up by numerous Islamic scholars. And he was probably right. But what gets to me is the absolute backward thinking of these clerics. Night is day. Exploding yourself into bloody bits is not suicide.

I thought it would be amusing to see what exactly Muumen, a man who preaches suicide bombings, considers to be terrorism.

"Our interpretation of terror is obviously different from yours," he stated as I braced myself for this one.

"In Islam terror is mentioned and Muslims are invited to terrify the enemies of Allah. I understand that in your vision we are terrorists but in our vision we are fighters or persons who use terror according to the Islamic definition."

Nearly making me sick, Muumen told me all Israelis are military targets since they all must serve in the army: "Muslims in general have the right to carry out attacks even when they know that civilians of the enemy, even women and children, will be killed exactly like the enemy kills women and children on our side."

I immediately corrected Muumen's lies that Israel targets women and children but with a straight face he shoved conspiracy theories at me that the Israeli prime minister directs his military to take out Palestinian babies.

I asked Muumen why doesn't he strap on a suicide belt and blow himself up if it's the best way to achieve paradise. Why doesn't he send his children to become martyrs?

"When you speak in such heat and passion about young kids and teenagers, do not think I feel embarrassed. You should see the age of Israelis who serve in the army. Come and see the guys who are in the checkpoints, who kill, who chase our people. Aren't they young people of eighteen years old?"

He continued by lying to me.

"None of our martyrs who carried out suicide attacks was less than twenty years old and you should know that these young are the pioneers and leaders in their faith, their religious conscious and their understanding of our religion" he said.

Islamic Jihad has sent many bombers below the age of twenty to carry out attacks.

Muumen told me Islam "calls us and pushes us to scarify ourselves for Allah and for the religion. So we don't hesitate to encourage our children to follow the road of *jihad*."

As an American Jew who believes in the right of Israel to exist I asked the good *sheikh* whether I should be suicide bombed.

It's a question I dreaded asking, but I felt compelled.

Muumen responded that I should indeed be targeted in a suicide operation.

"American Jews are here as part of the Zionist plot against our people and against Islam and they deserve to be attacked, persecuted, and killed like the occupiers, the other Israeli Jews. If you would express your opposition to Zionism and to occupation, we will respect you and will express our sorrow if you were suicide bombed. But since this is not the case and you support Israel you should be killed," Muumen said.

The simplicity of his statement sent chills down my spine.

I asked the *sheikh* what he thought about Judaism. Did he believe if I followed the laws of the Torah I would merit heaven just like Ahmed would as a martyr?

Muumen accused Jews of falsifying the Torah. He claimed Judaism is based on "fake books" in which biblical stories were changed around to state Jews, not Muslims, are the chosen people.

"Therefore Allah and his characters in the Quran are different from the characters of Allah like it is presented in your falsified Torah."

He said the original Torah dictated Abraham was willing to sacrifice his "favorite" son Ishmael, not Isaac, and that Ishmael was a great prophet who laid the foundations for Muhammad.

Muumen informed me I would not go to heaven unless I converted to Islam.

"A Jew who believes in the present Torah is a non-believer who cannot be accepted into heaven. In order to enter heaven you should be Muslim," he said. "Jews are condemned to hell."

CHAPTER FOUR

NO JEWS IS GOOD NEWS

TERRORISTS' MEMORIES FUZZY WHEN IT COMES TO RECORDED HISTORY

*Then Solomon began to build the house of the Lord at Jerusalem in
mount Moriah, where the Lord appeared unto David his father, in the
place that David had prepared in the threshing floor of Ornan the
Jebusite. And he began to build in the second day of the second month,
in the fourth year of his reign. Now these are the things wherein
Solomon was instructed for the building of the house of God. The length
by cubits after the first measure was threescore cubits, and the breadth
twenty cubits…And he garnished the house with precious stones for
beauty: and the gold was gold of Parvaim. He overlaid also the house,
the beams, the posts, and the walls thereof, and the doors thereof, with
gold; and graved cherubims on the walls.*

Chronicle II

ABOUT YOUR SO-CALLED two Jewish Temples, they never
existed," said Sheikh Taysir Tamimi, chief Palestinian Justice
and one of the most influential Muslim clerics in the Middle East.

With a straight face, the prominent *sheikh* sat there and explained to me very sternly there is no Jewish historic connection
whatsoever to the Temple Mount or Jerusalem; the Jewish Temples are a Zionist conspiracy; the Western Wall really was a tying
post for Muhammad's horse; and Islam's stated third holiest site,

the Al Aqsa Mosque, which has sprung multiple leaks and needs regular repainting, was built by Allah's angels.

I met Tamimi at his luxurious, well-decorated office in a poor Arab neighborhood on the outskirts of Jerusalem. Tamimi isn't some wacko preacher in the Gaza Strip; he's considered the second most important Palestinian cleric after Muhammad Hussein, the Grand Mufti of Jerusalem. Tamimi regularly preaches from the Al Aqsa Mosque. He represents Muslim thinking in the West Bank and Gaza.

I have no hesitation about including Tamimi in a book about my conversations with terrorists since he regularly promotes so-called martyrdom, convincing young Palestinians they will go to paradise for blowing themselves up among targeted civilians. During out meeting, Tamimi gave me a long lecture about the importance of suicide bombings.

According to Tamimi, the history of the Jewish people and our ties to the Temple Mount are forgeries.

"Israel started since 1967 making archeological digs to show Jewish signs to prove the relationship between Judaism and the [Temple Mount] and they found nothing," Tamimi said, ignoring all evidence confirmed by every respectable archeologist in the world today.

The Temple Mount is the holiest site in Judaism.

Just a brief rundown of my religion's most sacred place: The First Jewish Temple was built by King Solomon in the tenth century B.C. It was destroyed by the Babylonians in 586 B.C. The Second Temple was rebuilt in 515 B.C. after Jerusalem was freed from Babylonian captivity. That temple was destroyed by the Roman Empire in A.D. 70. Each temple stood for a period of about four centuries.

The Jewish Temple was the center of religious Jewish worship. It housed the Holy of Holies, which contained the Ark of the Covenant and was said to be the area upon which G-d's *shechina* or "presence" dwelt. All Jewish holidays centered on worship at the Temple. The Jewish Temples served as the primary location for the offering of sacrifices and was the main gathering place for the Jewish people.

According to the Talmud, the world was created from the foundation stone of the Temple Mount. It's believed to be the Biblical Mount Moriah, the location where Abraham fulfilled G-d's test to see if he would be willing to sacrifice his son Isaac. Jewish tradition holds Mashiach, or the Jewish Messiah, will return and rebuild the third and final Temple on the holy Mount in Jerusalem.

The Kotel, or Western Wall, is the one part of the Temple Mount that survived the destruction of the Second Temple and still stands today in Jerusalem.

The Temple Mount has remained a focal point for Jewish services for thousands of years. Prayers for a return to Jerusalem and the rebuilding of the Jewish Temple have been uttered by Jews since the Second Temple was destroyed, according to Jewish tradition. Throughout all notorious Jewish exiles, the Jews never gave up their hope of returning to Jerusalem and reestablishing their Temple. To this day Jews worldwide pray facing the Western Wall, while Muslims turn their backs away from the Temple Mount and pray toward Mecca.

But Tamimi says all this well-documented Jewish history is hogwash.

"Jews declared they dug and dug for proof that their imaginary Temples existed and they didn't find any sign. Nothing. We don't want to throw you into the sea but we say you are making us [Muslims] very upset with these lies about your Temples," Tamimi told me.

What was this guy talking about? I called him out immediately.

Aside from all the textual evidence affirming the Temples— the detailed descriptions of Temple specifications and construction in the Bible; letters and writings from the Roman Empire, the works of first-century Jewish historian Josephus, a wealth of epigraphic writings, among other things—the evidence of the Jewish Temples is etched in the land.

Excavations on the Temple Mount were always difficult due to Muslim objections, but key discoveries were still made the past 150 years. Digs by Sir Charles William Wilson, an officer of the British Royal Engineers, produced an important arch, mentioned by Josephus "as having connected the Upper City of Jerusalem with the sacred compound during the Second Temple Period."

Professor Binyamin Mazar of Hebrew University found important potsherds with Temple references; a large number of ritual baths; a staircase of monumental dimensions which led up to large gates in the southern wall of the Temple compound; a massive plaza where pilgrims were said to have congregated before entering the Temple precincts after purifying themselves in the ritual baths of a building in the center of the plaza, which was found at the same time.

Temple Mount dirt nearly thrown out by the Waqf, the Muslim custodians of the Mount, contained Jewish Temple artifacts.

Mazar's daughter, Eilat, is one of the lead archeologists at the City of David, one of the most important archeological finds of modern times. The site is located on the southeastern hill to the south of the Temple Mount, and is believed to be the area used by David to conquer Jerusalem and build his palace. One can literally take out the Bible and read exact descriptions of the place, which has yielded many finds, including Temple Period artifacts, synagogues, a tower at which Solomon was believed to have been anointed king, and recently what may be the largest ritual bath in the world in the area leading up to the Mount. Jews needed to dip in a ritual bath before ascending the Temple Mount. New Temple period discoveries are made at the City of David almost every month.

I pointed all these facts out to Tamimi, but he denied everything.

"I disagree with you. If anything was discovered, Israel would have made a big deal that it found something. The only thing they discovered were Arab and Islamic things," Tamimi told me.

"What you are saying is total fabrication," I told Tamimi, actually laughing in his face, although I tried to respond in a respectful manner.

"There was no Jewish civilization in Jerusalem," Tamimi retorted. "Many people lived here throughout the ages and they left some artifacts, but so what? There is no proof of any Jews being here."

"How can you make such a claim? Israel just last week announced it found intact a Second Temple period Jewish neighborhood near Jerusalem, with Jewish artifacts, including Jewish ritual baths and a synagogue. These finds happen all the time. Our history is written in the land. How can you deny this?" I said frankly.

During the course of our conversation I upset Tamimi several times by pointing out his lies and distortions in a very direct way. An Israel-based media network learned I was going to interview Tamimi and had sent along a camera crew to film our confrontation. Afterwards, I asked the network to mainly use only Tamimi's responses and not my questions because I didn't want viewers to see I could barely keep a straight face. I was astonished by the level of ridiculousness spewed by the good *sheikh* and just couldn't look directly at him in a serious way. I am usually able to keep my composure during these kinds of interviews, but this time I just couldn't do that.

My translator Ali later told me there were several points at which Tamimi was ready to depart in the middle of the interview. At first I thought this was an exaggeration. But I looked at the footage and saw indeed Tamimi tried to get up from his chair four times. I was so engrossed in the conversation while it was taking place I didn't notice.

Tamimi's staff had been alerted to the debate being waged with a visiting Jew. Before I knew it we had an audience of about a dozen people, most of whom looked visibly amazed I was challenging their respected leader. Some were shaking their heads in disagreement almost every time I opened my mouth. One mean-looking guy gave the impression he wanted to jump me.

"These archeological things you cite are lies," continued Tamimi. "Jews came to the [Temple area] in 1967 and not before."

As extremist as Tamimi sounds, he should not be taken lightly. He represents the thinking of a large number of Muslims in the Middle East, who have come the past few dozen years to believe the Temple Mount is theirs only and that the Jewish Temples never existed.

Not all Muslims worldwide deny documented Jewish history, but it is a growing phenomenon in the Middle East. Muslims previously traditionally acknowledged the Temple Mount is holy to the Jews. Some of the most important early Islamic scholars wrote the Al Aqsa Mosque was built at the site of Solomon's Temple. Even initial Palestinian leaders recognized the Mount as being the site of Solomon's Temples. But the Palestinian Authority the past twenty or so years led an effective campaign to delegitimize all Jewish ties to Israel. Many prominent Western Muslim leaders try to counteract the growing trend of Jewish Temple-denial, but so many in the Middle East believe their leaders, who change things around to make Islam the only legitimate actor. They call the mount the Haram Al-Sharif.

The absurd denial of the Jewish Temples is of course shared by the terrorists, many of whom were offended that I even asked whether the Jewish Temples existed.

"We are fed up with this crap nonsense of the Temple Mount," said Nasser Abu Aziz, the deputy commander of the Al Aqsa Martyrs Brigades in the northern West Bank. "We do not know where this story came from. There is no historical or archeological proof that this legendary Temple existed. We are sick of this story. But Allah warned us that Jews will look for an excuse in order to corrupt life on earth, so we are not surprised from the fact that you keep raising this issue."

Muhammad Abdul-El, spokesman for the Popular Resistance Committees terror organization, told me the Jewish Temples "existed only in your dreams. Go look for your stupid Temple elsewhere. And I am not saying this for political reasons. I say that the enemy invented this story in order to justify its occupation of Jerusalem."

Abu Abdullah, considered one of the most important operational members of Hamas's so-called military wing, accused all Jews of being pathological liars.

"Stop lying and believing your own lies. Even if there was such a thing [as a Jewish Temple] do you really believe that Solomon, who was a prophet, would have built a Temple in the place that Allah wanted for the Al Aqsa Mosque?"

The Al Aqsa Mosque was constructed around A.D. 709 to serve as a shrine near another shrine, the Dome of the Rock, which was built by an Islamic *caliph*. Al Aqsa was meant to mark the place where Muslims came to believe Muhammad ascended to heaven.

Islamic tradition states Muhammad took a journey in a single night from "a sacred mosque"—believed to be in Mecca in southern Saudi Arabia—to "the farthest mosque," and from a rock there ascended to heaven to receive revelations from Allah that became part of the Quran. The farthest mosque later became associated with Jerusalem, which is not mentioned once in the Quran.

According to Tamimi, the Western Wall, which predates the Al Aqsa Mosque by almost one thousand years, is really part of Al Aqsa.

"The Western wall is the western wall of the Al Aqsa Mosque," Tamimi said.

He said the Western Wall is properly called the Al-Boraq Wall, which he explained was where Muhammad tied his horse, named Boraq, before ascending to heaven.

"It's where Prophet Muhammad tied his animal which took him from Mecca to Jerusalem to receive the revelations of Allah," Tamimi told me.

It would be one thing if Mideast Muslims simply go around denying history. But they dangerously take it one step further and attempt to physically erase Jewish history.

In the late 1990s, the Temple Mount Muslim Waqf custodians excavated parts of the mount alongside Solomon's Stables, an area directly underneath the southeastern corner of the Temple Mount. The area had been called Solomon's Stables since Crusader times, when it was used by the Crusaders as horse stables.

As they do with so many other Jewish holy sites, Mideast Muslims in 1996 converted the Stables area in a huge mosque—one of the largest in the world, capable of accommodating up to seven thousand worshipers.

In 1997, the Waqf commenced illegal excavations, causing major damage to the eastern and southern sections of the Western

Wall and digging up tons of invaluable dirt thought to contain First and Second Jewish Temple artifacts.

After removing and hijacking important large artifacts, the Waqf quickly disposed of truckloads of the priceless Temple dirt but were halted by Israeli authorities who helped transfer the soil to a safe place outside the Mount where archeologists were able to sift through the ruins. Jewish Temple relics were indeed found, including coins with Hebrew writing referencing the Temple, part of a Hasmonean lamp, several other Second Temple lamps, Temple period pottery with Jewish markings, a marble pillar shaft, and other Temple period artifacts.

The Waqf was widely accused of disposing of the important dirt in a malicious attempt to destroy evidence of any Jewish presence on the Temple Mount, and indeed this is absolutely what I believe they were trying to do.

I made no bones about bringing these accusations up with Tamimi, who has major influence over the direction of the Waqf.

"You guys were absolutely trying to dispose of Jewish history," I charged. "It would have been a travesty for the Waqf if Jewish Temple artifacts were found during Muslim excavations."

Just like everything else, Tamimi denied archeologists found Temple relics in the dirt.

He went on to claim the Al Aqsa Mosque was "built by the angels forty years after the building of Al-Haram in Mecca. This we have no doubt is true."

That the mosque was built by angels is a common theme in the Muslim world. It was repeated during an interview I conducted with Sheik Kamal Hatib, vice chairman of the Islamic Movement, the Muslim group in Israel most identified with the Temple Mount. Only Hatib predated the Al Aqsa Mosque all the way to the creation of man:

> We the Muslims believe that Al Aqsa was built since the time of Adam—Allah bless him. Al Aqsa was built by the angels as it is mentioned in a verse of the Quran. The mosque is mentioned in the Quran, which speaks about the raising of the prophet.

I asked Tamimi if Jerusalem is so important to Islam why isn't it mentioned once in the Quran. I pointed out it's mentioned over seven hundred times in the Hebrew Bible.

Lying to me about his own religion's holy book, Tamimi said, "Jerusalem is in the Quran. It's mentioned in the first *sura* of the Quran."

This is absolutely not true. Jerusalem is not directly mentioned in the Quran, only in the *hadith*, or oral traditions relating to the words and deeds of Muhammad that were written over one hundred years after Muhammad's death. Many Islamic scholars say the Quran alludes to Jerusalem.

Regarding Jerusalem being mentioned numerous times in my Bible, Tamimi said the Torah was "falsified by the Jews. We don't believe in all your versions. The Torah as revealed to our Prophet Moses never once mentioned the Temple or Jerusalem."

He went on to accuse Israel of trying to destroy the Al Aqsa Mosque, which is one of the most outrageous claims anyone can make, but is repeated so often it's taken as fact by so many Middle East Muslims and many times even parroted by my colleagues in the news media.

Tamimi and his ilk regularly use Judaism's holiest site for Palestinian and pan-Arab political gain. Time and again the Palestinians use mythical Israeli threats against Al Aqsa to stir up the masses into a violent revolt. The Temple Mount is one of the most sensitive spots in the universe. Arab terror wars have been waged using the mosque as provocation while the Muslims are the only ones causing damage to the Temple Mount.

In September 2000, following the collapse of U.S.-mediated Israeli-Palestinian peace talks, Ariel Sharon, then the Israeli opposition leader, famously visited the Temple Mount in what was used by the Palestinians as a provocation against the Al Aqsa Mosque. Young Palestinian men who were curiously strategically placed following Sharon's visit came running out of the mosque hurling rocks at Jewish worshipers below at the Western Wall platform. Israeli police rushed to the scene. Violent clashes ensued.

The Palestinian propaganda machine went into overdrive, broadcasting messages Israel was trying to take over the Al Aqsa

Mosque, and thus was born the *intifada*, or Palestinian terror war led by Yasser Arafat to take Palestine from the Jews by force. Arafat actually called his war the Al Aqsa Intifada.

But later, Palestinian terror leaders and Arafat officials admitted they used Sharon's visit to the Mount as pretext and that the violence had nothing at all to do with any purported Israeli threats to the Al Aqsa Mosque.

"Whoever thinks the *Intifada* broke out because of the despised Sharon's visit to the Al-Aqsa Mosque is wrong…This *Intifada* was planned in advance, ever since President Arafat's return from the Camp David negotiations," admitted Palestinian Communications Minister 'Imad Al-Faluji to an Arab newspaper.

Arafat himself spoke of planning the *intifada* months before Sharon's visit, as did Marwan Barghouti, a jailed Palestinian terrorist and one of the chief architects of the *intifada*. (I believe Barghouti will eventually be freed by Israel to become a future Palestinian leader.) Multiple senior terror leaders involved in *intifada* planning freely admitted to me on numerous occasions Sharon's visit to the Mount had little to do with the *intifada*.

Yet many news reporters to this day ignore the *intifada* planners own glaring admissions and regularly claim the 2000 violence was sparked by Sharon's visit to the Temple Mount.

The theme of using nonexistent Israeli threats against the Al Aqsa Mosque is repeated often. During the time of my interview with Tamimi, Israel was conducting routine renovation work near the Temple Mount to replace a ramp that provides access to a gate leading to the Mount. The work schedule was coordinated with Arab leaders. The renovations took place in full view of a twenty-four-hour-a-day Web camera, and were not on the Mount itself. All logic dictates the work in question couldn't have possibly affected the Al Aqsa Mosque. Still, Tamimi and Muslim leaders worldwide claimed Israel was trying to weaken the foundations of the Mount and collapse the Al Aqsa Mosque. Muslims threatened violence. News media reported some of the crazy Palestinian claims as fact. Cowardly, the mayor of Jerusalem postponed construction of the new gate.

To his face I accused Sheikh Tamimi of "using the Al Aqsa Mosque time and time again as a political tool to rev up the masses. You are going in the mosque and preaching these lies. And Muslims believe you and start violence."

Insulted by my directness, the *sheikh* got visibly agitated.

"I'm using the mosque to start riots? On the contrary, Israel is damaging the Al Aqsa Mosque. Sharon's visit provoked the Palestinians."

I have to hand it to Tamimi and to the greater Middle East Muslim world, I have respect for one thing—at least they care about the Al Aqsa Mosque, even if some only use it as pretense for political gain. I wish Jewish leaders cared enough about the Temple Mount to work up the Jewish masses about nonexistent threats. I wish Jews cared enough about the Temple Mount to counter the Muslim claims of exclusivity. But my fellow Jews have shamefully forfeited their holiest site, the Temple Mount.

Temple Mount: No Prayer Zone…Unless You're Muslim

It was a sunny, mild February morning in Jerusalem. My brother Josh and I met early to attend synagogue services and immerse in a *mikveh*, or Jewish ritual bath, as is required by Jewish law before ascending the Temple Mount.

Currently, some rabbis forbid Jews to go up to the mount until the Third Temple is built even though there are records of Jews, including some of the most prominent Jewish law scholars, visiting the Temple ruins during the Byzentine period and beyond. Other contemporary rabbinic authorities permit entry to the outer areas of the Mount, which can be measured by a change in the kind of foundation stone.

According to Jewish law, the sanctity of the Temple Mount is structured in concentric circles. In the innermost circles, where the Holy of Holies was said to be located, the restrictions of access are the greatest. During Temple times, only the *kohen gadal*, or high priest, was allowed to enter the most restricted area, and this happened once a year on Yom Kipper. The outer layers are less restricted.

Josh and I met our tour guide, Nachman Kupietsky, at exactly 7:30 a.m. at the gate leading to the Temple Mount. The holiest Jewish site, you see, is open to Jews and Christian only on Sundays through Thursdays from 7:30 a.m. to 10:00 a.m. and 12:30 p.m. to 1:30 p.m., and not on any Christian, Jewish, or Muslim holidays or other days considered "sensitive" by the Muslim Waqf custodians. It's open to Muslims nearly 24-7.

After Israel recaptured eastern sections of Jerusalem, including the Temple Mount in the 1967 Six Day War, one of the first acts of Moshe Dayan, chief of staff of the Israeli Defense Forces, was to ensure Jordan and Muslim leaders the holiest site in Judaism would remain under Islamic custodianship. Jordan had controlled the area from 1948 to 1967, destroying nearby Jewish synagogues and graveyards. According to some records, Dayan personally removed an Israeli flag hoisted on the Temple Mount by Israeli soldiers in the aftermath of the war. The Mount was placed under the custodianship of the Waqf, which had and still has very strong ties to Jordan.

The Temple Mount was opened off and on to the general public until September 2000, when the Palestinians started their *intifada* by throwing stones at Jewish worshipers after Sharon's visit to the area. Following the onset of violence, the new, anti-religious Sharon government closed the Mount to all non-Muslims, using checkpoints to control all pedestrian traffic for fear of further clashes with the Palestinians.

The Temple Mount was reopened to non-Muslims in August 2003, but only for a few hours a day and under heavy guidelines for fear Jewish visits may agitate the Muslims and restart clashes.

The decision to reopen the Temple Mount fueled a wave of anti-Israeli incitement in the Palestinian press and a campaign by Arafat to have the area closed. Arafat at the time sent letters to Arab leaders threatening "grave consequences" for the "invasion of extremists disguised as tourists, under the auspices of the Israeli police."

Mahmoud Abbas, now Palestinian Authority president, called Jewish tours of the Mount "provocative." Arab League

Secretary General Amr Moussa said the Christian and Jewish visits were "an insult to Muslims everywhere."

Currently, under Israeli authority, non-Muslims can go up but are ridiculously banned from praying on the Temple Mount. Non-Muslim visitors to the Mount must enter from a particular gate, usually with a guided tour. Visitors pass a set of guidelines written in Hebrew and English on a large blue sign. These Israeli-enforced rules state "Holy objects not permitted." The rules dictate non-Muslims cannot pray on the Mount. Visitors are banned from entering any of the mosques without direct Waqf permission. Rules are enforced by Waqf agents, who watch tours closely and alert nearby Israeli police to any breaking of their guidelines.

Israeli police units screen visitors and strongly suggest Jewish men do not wear their *kipas*, or scull caps, on the Mount. That's right. In the Jewish state, Jewish police ask Jews to remove their religious Jewish *kipas* before ascending the holiest site in Judaism for fear of offending the Muslims. It's absolute madness.

Our guide Kupietsky was an Orthodox Jew who usually wears a *kipa* but covers his head with a baseball cap while on the Mount. My brother Josh and I and several other Jewish male visitors showed up wearing our *kipas*. Like the Jews who obligingly marched into Nazi gas chambers without a trace of resistance, the Jewish men on our Temple Mount tour removed their *kipas* before passing through a Mount checkpoint, dutifully donning their baseball caps lest a Muslim see a religious Jew on the Temple Mount.

Josh and I refused to take our *kipas* off. I would go to jail under torture before surrendering my Jewish identity to anyone, especially to other Jews who cowardly enforce self-hating, anti-Jewish laws enacted by religion-loathing Israeli leaders.

Kupietsky gave Josh and me problems, arguing we should remove our *kipas* to continue.

"Over my dead body," I said.

"No way in hell," said Josh.

I heard other Jews on our tour whispering about the two Jews who shouldn't be making trouble. They complained we were holding up the group.

"Just take your *kipa* off," one of the Jewish men told us.

After a few minutes of argument in which it was clear we wouldn't budge, Kupietsky finally agreed to let Josh and I remain with his tour while wearing our *kipas*. I first had to flash my press credentials and threaten to write about the treatment I was receiving for being Jewish, which I did anyway. The Israeli police at the checkpoint weren't happy, but they didn't want to mess with a reporter. They let us up. I ascended the Temple Mount proudly, as a Jew should.

Our tour was followed every step of the way by a Waqf official, who was paying particularly close attention probably after being warned by the Israelis two potential troublemakers were on their way.

Once on the Mount, Kupietsky told Josh and I we were lucky we got up with our *kipas*. He said Orthodox guests who decide to wear *kipas* are routinely delayed by Israeli police at the entrance to the Temple Mount for up to thirty minutes while they are interrogated about the purpose of their visit.

Kupietsky told the group of an instance in which an elderly Jewish woman was detained by the Israelis last summer for putting her head down while sitting on a bench on the Mount:

> It was a hot day and she just wanted to rest for a few minutes. The Waqf started screaming and the police arrested her. They thought she was praying. She told me she was held for six hours and had to sign documents stating she would never again return to the Temple Mount.
>
> You also can't bring anything with Hebrew letters, even secular Hebrew books. The Waqf confiscated many of my tour books. One time I brought a guy who pulled out the Hebrew edition of the [Jerusalem] Post, and they took that from him.

The tour began with Kupietsky showing the area directly behind the Western Wall, the section used by Palestinians to start their *intifada* against Israel. Visitors were then brought to the steps of the Dome of the Rock and Al Aqsa Mosque.

Two Christians on the tour tried to enter Al Aqsa, but rejoined the group minutes later saying a Palestinian in worship garb slammed the doors and told them to go away.

Kupietsky took out a picture book to show the disappointed Christians images of the interior sections of the mosque, but a Waqf official who had been watching the tour demanded Israeli police confiscate the book, assuming it contained prayers. A scuffle ensued between the police, the cleric, and Kupietsky, but it was finally determined the book contained no Hebrew lettering and thus could not have been meant, gasp, for Jewish prayer.

Anti-Jewish laws surrounding the Mount are enforced by Israel not only on the site itself, but also adjacent to it. I'll never forget the time a Jewish man was removed by Israeli police from a key section of the Western Wall for blowing the *shofar*, or ceremonial ram's horn, during prayer services for the Rosh Hashanah high holiday, during which sounding the *shofar* is required. I personally broke the story.

Nineteen-year-old Jerusalem resident Eliyahi Kleiman was taken forcibly from the Western Wall during Rosh Hashanah of 2006 for fear the sound of the *shofar* would offend nearby Muslims congregating on the Temple Mount, which is opposite the wall. Kleiman had no previous arrest record and was not associated with any extremist or Temple Mount activist group.

Kleiman and about twenty Jews had gathered for Rosh Hashanah services at the northern-most section of the Western Wall commonly referred to as the "Small Wall." The little-known area stands opposite the spot at which the Holy of Holies is believed to have resided and is considered by Jews to be the most holy section of the Western Wall. The "Small Wall" is located within a mixed Jewish and Arab section of Jerusalem and is supposed to be accessible to Jews at all times.

Large prayer services take place at the central section of the Western Wall, where thousands gather for prayers on holidays. Smaller groups regularly gather at the "Small Wall."

Kleiman told me he had attended Rosh Hashanah services at the "Small Wall" annually for several years without incident. He said he prefers the smaller wall because it is less crowded.

After Kleiman began blowing the *shofar* during the Rosh Hashanah service, a nearby police officer asked him to stop, according to Kleiman, the Jerusalem police and several witnesses I spoke to.

Kleiman says he continued blowing for about two minutes to finish the section of prayer that requires the sounding of the *shofar*. Fifteen policemen immediately dragged Kleiman from the site, observers said.

Kleiman was going to be banned by the police from returning to the Western Wall or Temple Mount for the remainder of the Jewish holiday season, but the ban order was lifted, perhaps because I gave the case some publicity.

Shmulik Ben Ruby, a spokesman for the Jerusalem Police Authority, admitted to me the only reason Kleiman was removed from the Wall was Israel's fear of offending Muslims with the sound of the Jewish *shofar*.

"Hundreds of Muslims went up to the Temple Mount. In order to prevent any tensions between the two sides, we asked Kleiman to stop blowing the *shofar*," Ben Ruby said. "He continued and so he was removed and detained."

A Jew in Israel today can't even blow the *shofar* on a high Jewish holiday at our holy sites. Meanwhile, Muslims, who have full rights to the Temple Mount, are about as loud as it gets. Several times per day the Muslims broadcast prayer services on loudspeakers that can be heard for miles, including every morning at about 5 a.m. It is extremely disturbing to many Jews nearby, but you don't hear the Jews complain about it. During the Muslim holy month of Ramadan, Arabs in Jerusalem's Old City regularly celebrate after sunset with loud explosions from firecrackers and gunshot blanks. But Allah forbid a Jew once a year for a few minutes blows the *shofar* near the Temple Mount.

And it infuriates me to no end in the Jewish state Jews cannot pray on the Temple Mount. Perhaps set up this way intentionally, most groups associated with the Temple Mount that are getting major publicity in Israel consist of right-wing nut cases who make extremist statements about taking over the Al Aqsa Mosque. Advocating for Jewish rights on the holiest Jewish site has sadly become a fringe, extremist cause. It's sickening. Many Jews nowadays have no pride whatsoever; especially the leadership of Israel. They are all afraid of asserting Jewish power in any way, worried what the Muslims might do and what the international community might think.

Well, if believing Jews have the right to pray on the Temple Mount is an extremist cause, call me extremist. I am not advocating expelling Muslims. I'm not advocating removing any mosques from the Mount. But it's our holiest site; why the hell can't we pray there? One Israeli lawmaker has proposed building a synagogue on the Mount. He has been lambasted by fellow Jews. What in the world is wrong with a synagogue on the Mount? Miamonidies built one once. It will of course never happen; the terrorists will start World War III. They told me as much.

"If anybody other than Muslims dares to pray on the [Mount] this will cause a war. The world will not be the same anymore if such an aggression will take place. We will not allow anybody to desecrate this blessed area," said the Committees' Muhammad Abel-El.

Al Aqsa Brigades northern West Bank deputy commander Nasser Abu Aziz threatened if Jews assert their rights to pray on the Mount:

> This will cause a huge explosion, a third Intifada, a war. We, and I believe all Muslims from all the world, will react in launching attacks, suicide attacks, rockets from inside the Palestinian territories and missiles from outside. I think that this will bring the collapse of the Arab regimes that are so crucial to the maintenance of the state of Israel. I do not know if I can imagine all that will happen.

Muslim Mount leader accepts reality!

Not all Palestinian Muslim leaders deny Jewish history. Deep inside Jerusalem's Old City, down the narrow stone streets of the Muslim Quarter, I found a true gem, a former Waqf official who defies his former colleagues, the custodians of the Temple Mount, and admits the First and Second Jewish Temples existed and stood at the current location of the Al Aqsa Mosque. The man divulged in a rare meeting Al Aqsa custodians passed down stories for centuries from generation to generation indicating the mosque was built at the site of the former Jewish temples.

I was put in touch with the former Waqf official by Palestinian elements who occasionally work alongside Israel on holy site and other issues. I was told I could only meet the former Temple Mount custodian if I didn't use his name, even though it will likely be easy for those in the know to identify him. The man, in his late sixties, was dismissed from his Waqf position after he quietly made his beliefs known.

The former Waqf official and I talked over tea in his home, a small Old City apartment not far from the Temple Mount. The dining room was modestly decorated, the walls littered with framed verses of the Quran. Pictures and small-scale models of the Al Aqsa Mosque were everywhere.

It was very brave of the man to meet me. He said an on-the-record interview would endanger his life. He spoke quietly but also very confidently, and made me feel welcome in his home.

He said the Muslim denial of the existence of the Jewish temples is political in nature and is not rooted in facts.

"Prophet Solomon built his famous Temple at the same place that later the Al Aqsa Mosque was built. It cannot be a coincidence that these different holy sites were built at the same place. The Jewish Temple Mount existed," he said.

"I am mentioning historical facts," said the former leader. "I know that the traditional denial about the temple existing at the same place as Al Aqsa is more a political denial. Unfortunately our religious and political leaders chose the option of denial to fight the Jewish position and demands regarding Al Aqsa and taking back the Temple Mount compound. In my opinion we should admit the truth and abandon our traditional position."

I couldn't believe what I was hearing. A Waqf official who actually accepts reality?

The man related to me stories he said were passed for centuries among Al Aqsa Mosque custodians.

"[The existence of the Jewish Temple at the site is obvious] according to studies, researches and archaeological signs that we were also exposed to. But especially according to the history that passed from one Muslim generation to another—we believe Al Aqsa was built on the same place where the Temple of the Jews—the first monotheistic religion—existed."

He outlined some of the stories related to him:

> We learned that the Christians, especially those who believed that Jesus was crucified by the Jews, used to throw their garbage at the Temple Mount site. They used to throw the pieces of cotton and other material Christian women used in cleaning the blood of their monthly cycle. Doing so they believed that they were humiliating, insulting and harming the Jews at their holiest site. This way they are hurting them like Jews hurt Christians when crucifying Jesus.

> It is known also that most of the first guards of the Al Aqsa Mosque when it was built were Jews. The Muslims knew at that time that they could not find any more loyal and faithful than the Jews to guard the mosque and its compound. They knew that the Jews have a special relation with this place.

But the former senior Waqf leader said the Jewish temples have "lost their purpose."

"As we are the religion here to correct everything that was before us there is no need for the Temple. Allah chose Islam as its final and favorite religion."

He stressed although the Temples existed, the Mount rightfully belongs to the Muslims and that Jews have no right to pray there and should not even visit. Even the good Waqf personalities demand Muslim exclusivity.

I told terror-supporter Tamimi about my meeting with the former Waqf official. Tamimi denounced the man as an "Israeli collaborator. Who paid off this man? I set the rules for the Waqf and the Muslims and I told you the Temples never existed."

For Tamimi and for so many Muslims around the world, the centuries old battle for the Temple Mount has ended in victory.

CHAPTER FIVE

FROM RICHARD GERE TO ROSIE O' DONNELL, TERRORISTS ARE REALLY FONDA HOLLYWOOD

H I, I'M RICHARD GERE and I'm speaking for the entire world. We're with you during this election time," said a radiant Richard Gere, star of such films as *Pretty Woman*, *Primal Fear*, and *American Gigolo*.

"It's really important: get out and vote," continued the proud actor, his words simultaneously being translated into Arabic.

Then, switching to actually speaking in Arabic, Gere concluded in a strong American accent: "Take part in the election."

Gere was speaking in a commercial that was broadcast repeatedly on Palestinian television in January 2006, just prior to one of the first municipal Palestinian elections since late Palestinian terror leader Yasser Arafat held what was widely regarded as sham local elections about thirty years prior.

This time, Gere was urging Palestinians to vote in local ballots essentially split between the Hamas terrorist organization, responsible for dozens of suicide bombings, and the Fatah organization, responsible for dozens of suicide bombings.

Gere's co-stars in the commercial were Chief Palestinian Justice Taysir Tamimi and former Greek Orthodox Church spokesperson Atallah Hanna. Tamimi, featured prominently in this book, is a well-known terror supporter and justifier of suicide bombings who regularly delivers fiery sermons on Palestinian television calling for the downfall of America and Israel. Hanna was fired from his church position after being accused of directly aiding terror organizations. He has held public lovey-dovey meetings with leaders of Hamas and Hezbollah and appears regularly on Palestinian television urging children to blow themselves up. Among some of Gere co-star Hanna's televised gems: "We encourage our youth to participate in the resistance, to carry out martyrdom attacks."

Gere's appearance on Palestinian television was sponsored by "One Voice," a far-leftist organization run by an outspoken Israeli businessman.

Palestinians indeed took Gere's advice and voted *en masse*, electing Hamas legislators by a large margin. Hamas terrorists boasted their victory was in part fueled by Israel's retreat under fire from the Gaza Strip a few months earlier and the terror group's regular firing of rockets into Jewish population centers. Hamas officials stated they would use their election victory to lead the Palestinians in their jihad against the West and against Israel.

Abu Abdullah, considered one of the most important members of Hamas's so-called military wing, told me of Gere's appearance, "We thank Richard Gere for his efforts in the historic election of the Palestinian Islamic resistance [Hamas]."

Abdullah urged Gere to "tell your American government that they should respect the democratic choice of the Palestinians in the elections that Gere promoted and that they should stop undermining the legitimate government of Hamas."

Since I don't know Gere personally, I cannot determine whether he realized in his shallow, Botoxed brain he was urging voter turnout in elections between terror groups in one of the most terror-saturated societies the world has ever known. Whether he knew Hamas would utilize the legitimacy granted to them by the international community's support of elections, urged on by Gere, to demand foreign aid and worldwide diplomatic status for their terror organization.

When I was a kid growing up in a modern Orthodox Jewish household in Philadelphia, I used to observe Hollywood and the music industry with quiet amusement, watching as lamebrain celebrities involved themselves in causes they probably couldn't spell and made all sorts of pronouncements about issues they largely don't have the capacity to understand. There were also celebrities whom I thought did comprehend what they were doing, and I was baffled, but still unconcerned, as some openly sided with America's enemies and attempted to undermine our government's policies.

But it wasn't until I moved to the Middle East in February 2005 and started talking to terrorists that I fully realized just how much damage some of our "antiwar" celebrities are causing.

A lot of terrorists have satellite televisions and advanced communication equipment and are quite adept at browsing the Internet. In today's wired world, it's very easy for anyone speaking any language to be updated almost immediately about all kinds of events. This includes America's terror enemies, who pay particularly close attention to news of U.S. domestic opinion regarding our government's Mideast policies. They understand that in the U.S. the fight for public opinion is everything—change public opinion, get American citizens to lose their drive to fight and the government and military ultimately must change, as well. The terrorists time their attacks in part on the status of our national debate and on the American news cycle.

The terrorists want our war on terror to end and they believe they know how to end it. Every single terrorist that I talked to about Iraq pointed at some point during our conversation to the model of Vietnam, in which they said the U.S. was forced to retreat after domestic public approval for the war tanked. The terrorists told me they were aware of the important role Hollywood had in galvanizing opposition to Vietnam and that they are generally aware now multiple Hollywood heavyweights have been urging the U.S. to withdraw from Iraq and Afghanistan, create dialogue with Iran, and pressure Israel into handing more territory to the Palestinians.

Islamic terrorists loathe our culture; they told me they believe our movies and music are corrupting humanity on earth. They think U.S. actors and singers should be stoned to death for the negative influence they are having on Muslim youth around the world. But for the terrorists to win—and they openly state that for them winning means imposing a worldwide Islamic caliphate—the terrorists will accept any help offered and will take advantage of any tools they have at their disposal, apparently including Hollywood.

I put together a panalopy of Palestinian terror leaders and *schmoozed* with them about their thoughts on some of our outspoken celebrities; in some cases I read to them a series of celebrity quotes regarding various political issues, and the terrorists offered their critiques.

◇

No discussion about U.S. celebrities meddling in our foreign affairs can appropriately begin without two-time Academy Award-winning American actress, former fashion model, and fitness guru Jane Fonda. Star of numerous films, most recently *Monster-in-Law,* and ex-wife of CNN founder Ted Turner, Fonda is most known for her political activism, particularly her opposition to the Vietnam War.

In 1970, Fonda formed an antiwar road show designed as an answer to Bob Hope's USO tour, visiting military towns along the West Coast with the goal of establishing a dialogue with soldiers to speak against their upcoming deployments to Vietnam. She moved on to speaking at antiwar rallies and spewing war crime accusations against the U.S. to National Liberation Front officials.

At the height of her Vietnam activism, in 1972, Fonda visited Hanoi and, among other statements, repeated unsubstantiated North Vietnamese claims America had been deliberately targeting the dike system along a major Vietnamese river. Fonda was photographed in Hanio seated on an anti-aircraft battery used against American aircrews and later participated in several radio broadcasts on behalf of the Communist regime, asking U.S. military men to consider the consequences of their actions.

When cases of torture by the Vietnamese began to emerge among POWs returning to the United States, Fonda called our returning American POWs "hypocrites and liars."

I talked with the terrorists about the legendary Fonda; most of them were aware of her anti-Vietnam war efforts, but did not know she was involved in current antiwar activities. The terrorists were thrilled to learn Fonda had spoken on behalf of Palestinians, and against the U.S. war in Iraq, traveling to Israel with the leftist group Peace Now, and talking at anti-Iraq war protests.

I read to the terrorists the following statement by Fonda at an anti–Iraq war rally:

> A lot of press people have been asking me today, "What's the difference between now and during the Vietnam war?" And I'll tell you one huge crucial difference: it took six years for Vietnam veterans, active-duty servicemen, Gold Star mothers and military families to come out against the war. It has happened now within three years of the war. Their presence here is critical, and we should acknowledge their courage.

Ala Senakreh, the chief in the West Bank of the Al Aqsa Martyrs Brigades terror organization, thanked Fonda for her "holy" efforts.

"We thank Fonda and we strengthen her and call upon her to continue in her efforts," said Senakreh. "I tell her that she must help her people to understand that the occupied people have the right to defend themselves. When Americans in Iraq and the Israelis in Palestine occupy our lands and rights and want to kill us, we do not offer them roses. We fight.

"I tell Fonda to tell the mothers of American soldiers that your sons are committing atrocities. Keep up your holy efforts, Jane Fonda, because it helps us and it helps peace."

Ramada Adassi, leader of the Al Aqsa Brigades in the Anskar refugee camp in the northern West Bank, said Fonda's speaking out against the Iraq war "proves that Americans are not only a group of barbarians and gangsters, but some, like Fonda, deserve to be thanked for their healthy sense, for their refusal to close their eyes behind the official propaganda."

Adassi told me he and some of his terror friends are hoping Fonda and some of her celebrity friends become more vocal.

"Thank you Mrs. Fonda and we hope you and your friends will succeed. We have been waiting to hear your voices and we hope you will succeed to prevent the big disaster that the pro-Zionists are planning."

I decided not to ask exactly what "disaster" he was referring to.

In September 2005, Fonda and controversial extreme leftist Scottish politician George Galloway, who in June 2007 threw me out of his office for calling Hamas a terror group during a radio interview, had planned a national bus tour against the war in Iraq, but postponed it due to a relief operation for the Gulf Coast, which had been devastated by Hurricane Katrina. Fonda then planned a second bus tour with her daughter in 2006 but scrapped those plans as well, stating she felt like she would distract attention from the activism of Cindy Sheehan, a bereaved mother whose son, Casey, was killed during his service in Iraq.

Sheehan first attracted international news media attention in August 2005 for her extended antiwar demonstration at a makeshift protest camp she created about three miles outside President Bush's Texas ranch. Sheehan organized multiple tours and rallies against the Iraq war, was arrested for protesting at Bush's May 2007 State of the Union Address, spoke out in Europe and South America and has made statements some critics say defend *jihad*.

Sheehan has called Bush "the biggest terrorist in the world" and "worse than Osama Bin Laden." In January 2007, the bereaved mother traveled to Cuba and called for the closure of the U.S. military prison in Guantanamo Bay.

The Palestinian terrorist leaders I spoke to were emboldened when they heard some of the particulars of Sheehan's activism.

I read to them quotes in which Sheehan called terrorists "freedom fighters," such as when she stated, "Iraq was not involved in 9/11, Iraq was not a terrorist state. But now that we have decimated the country, the borders are open, freedom fighters from other countries are going in, and they [the U.S. government] have created more violence by going to an Islamic country..."

Brigades leader Adassi told me, "This sincere woman says what we've been saying all these last years—Saddam never threatened America or its security...You [Sheehan] give us hope and you show us that there are different Americans than those whom we know."

The terrorists applauded and expressed signs of joy when they heard Sheehan blamed the Iraq war on the Zionists.

Sheehan once stated to the media: "Am I emotional? Yes, my first born was murdered. Am I angry? Yes, he was killed for lies and for a Neo-Con agenda to benefit Israel. My son joined the army to protect America, not Israel."

Brigades chieftain Senakreh replied to Sheehan's comments: "I agree with her completely and thank her from deep in my heart when she dares to tell the Americans that their children are killed for the interests of Israel.

"The American security has nothing to do with the atrocities in Iraq and in Palestine. I tell this noble mother that American soldiers and Israeli soldiers receive common training and share their experience in how to turn these atrocities even more cruel. You are losing your sons not for a better life for you, but for Israeli interests," Senakreh explained.

Abu Hamed, leader of the Al Aqsa Brigades in the northern Gaza Strip, urged Americans to listen to Sheehan.

"I hope that all the Americans will understand what this great mother understood. We hope you do not consider this mother as a humanitarian case who speaks from her own pain, because she is saying the truth. I hope you will take her as a good example."

Hamed's north Gaza terror cell is responsible for coordinating a lot of the rocket fire aimed from the northern Gaza Strip at nearby Jewish communities.

◇

When I chatted with the terrorists I got the sense that they were familiar with the general role outspoken celebrities have in America but they weren't too knowledgeable with some of our big-name actors and musicians. They had never heard of the Dixie Chicks, who strongly criticized Bush in the run up to the Iraq war. The terrorists didn't know who George Clooney was, although they were quite thrilled when I read to them some of Clooney's political statements, including a comment in which he referred to suicide bombers as "opponents" who resort to attacks because they "have no other war to win." (The terrorists, though, rejected Clooney's contention, explaining suicide bombers are motivated by the will to please Allah and reach paradise, and that suicide bombing is not at all a last resort, but the noblest way to achieve Heaven.)

The terrorists did not know about some recent American movies that have been criticized as anti-American and siding with *jihad*, such as Clooney's 2005 Academy Award winner *Syrianna*, which shows a cycle of Mideast violence that begins and ends with American oil interests. The terrorists weren't familiar with Oliver Stone's *World Trade Center*, which largely neglects to mention Islam, bin Laden, or Mohammed Atta and which some critics accused of putting forward a theory the American government and interests were responsible.

But one Hollywood actor whose activism the terrorists were familiar with is Academy Award winner Sean Penn. Actually, they didn't know Penn was an actor. The terrorists had no idea Penn starred in acclaimed films like *Mystic River* and *Dead Man Walking*, which humanized a killer on death row. They knew Penn only as the ex-husband of singer Madonna and thought he was famous in the U.S. for his marriage to the pop icon.

Madonna is probably the most well-known American celebrity in the Middle East. Everyone here has heard of her. The terrorists know Madonna because the singer is regularly referenced on religious Arab television networks for corrupting humanity on earth. When *sheikhs* cite samples of the U.S. attempting to pervert young Muslims with our demonic culture, they speak of Madonna.

Some of the terrorists I spoke to had heard Penn made speeches at anti–Iraq war rallies and knew the former Madonna husband embarked on solidarity visits to terror sanctuaries, such as his 2005 visit to Iran.

I had an entire speech Penn delivered in 2007 translated into Arabic for the terrorists' responses.

Here are some highlights of that Penn speech, remarks the actor proudly delivered at California Rep. Barbara Lee's March 24 "Town Hall Meeting" on the fourth anniversary of the invasion of Iraq:

Bush: You have broken our country and our hearts. The needless blood on your hands, and therefore, on our own, is drowning the freedom, the security, and the dream that America might have been once healed of and awakened by the tragedy of September 11, 2001. The verdict is in. You lied, connived, and exploited your own countrymen and most of all, our troops.

You, Misters Bush and Cheney; you, Ms. Rice, are villainously and criminally obscene people, obscene human beings, incompetent even to fulfill your own self-serving agenda. Iraq is not our toilet. They are a country of human beings whose lives, while once oppressed by Saddam, are now lived in Dante's inferno.

Now, because I've been on the streets of Baghdad during this occupational war, outside the Green Zone, without security, and you haven't, I've met children there. In that country of 25 million, these children have now suffered minimally, a rainstorm of civilian death around and among them totaling the equivalent of two hundred September 11ths in just four years of war. Two hundred 9/11s. Two hundred 9/11s.

Penn goes on to express solidarity with Iran, whose government is the largest state sponsor of terror worldwide—openly supporting Hamas, Islamic Jihad, and Hezbollah. Iran is accused of supporting the insurgency against U.S. troops in Iraq and of attempting to develop a nuclear weapons arsenal. Iranian President Mahmoud Ahmadinejad has stated numerous times he seeks to wipe Israel off the map.

"You want to rattle sabers toward Iran now?" asked Penn in the speech. "Let me tell you something about Iran, because I've been there and you haven't. Iran is a great country. A great country. Does it have its haters? You bet. Just like the United States has its haters. Just like the United States has a corrupt regime. Does it want a nuclear weapon? Maybe. Do we have one? You bet," stated Penn.

The terrorists absolutely loved Penn's speech.

"We feel deep respect for Penn and people like him that prove that America is not only the country that sponsors the Israeli terrorists and all evil forces in the world, but also a country of brave people who want a different policy based on justice and peace," said Senakreh.

North Gaza Brigades commander Abu Hamed called on Penn and Fonda to officially represent his terrorist organization to the world media: "I tell Penn and Fonda that we don't have the money that the Zionists have, therefore we don't own and we don't have access to your media, and we hope you would be those who will represent our pain and our cause," said Hamed.

Continued the enamored terrorist: "The Zionists and their allies in the U.S. did not hesitate to kill thousands of American civilians in the September 11 attacks just to justify their occupation in Afghanistan and in Iraq and their support to the Israelis. They rob these countries' economic resources and they are robbing our right for freedom. You Americans will pay the price and we hope these actors' messages will be understood by the American public."

Even though bin Laden personally took credit for 9/11, even though al-Qaida has openly boasted about their mega terror attack, September 11th is the one attack Palestinian terror leaders distance themselves from because they don't want to incur the wrath of the U.S. in such a big way.

Adassi explained Penn "understands very well that the Americans are drowning in the Iraqi mess. Bush scared the Americans with the weapons of mass destruction that Saddam Hussein supposedly had, and Penn understood that this lie was only an excuse in order to get rid of a leader that threatened Israel.

"I think Penn's words express dignity, express a deep humanitarian sense and this doesn't surprise me when it comes from an actor who has had to develop the sense of feeling. We hope Penn is somebody who can design a different public opinion. Penn must continue in his battle, which is very important because it is rare to see important people who criticize Bush, who is planning now to throw the American soldiers in the Iranian hell."

Adassi compelled all Americans to "[immediately] listen to Penn. Bush is leading you toward a bigger, much bigger disaster."

◇

While the terrorists didn't know much about most American movies, I wasn't very surprised when they told me they had heard of Steven Spielberg's 2005 Academy Award winning drama *Munich*, which depicts the Israeli government's secret retaliation for the 1972 Munich massacre of Israeli Olympic athletes by Arafat's Black September gunmen. The terrorists said although they hadn't seen the movie they were familiar with it since it deals with Palestinian "resistance" organizations and since the filmmakers, including writers Tony Kushner and Eric Roth, sought out and interviewed some Munich terrorists.

Until I came along, the terrorists assumed since Spielberg and Kushner are Jewish, the movie was one big Israeli propaganda piece, demonizing Black September and depicting the Israelis as victims.

But they were quite glad to hear Munich focused almost entirely on the Israeli response to Black September's operation—on Israel's assassinations of Black September members—and not on the massacre itself. I told them Spielberg and company boasted their movie was "balanced," presenting both sides as moral equivalents. I read to the terrorists a quote from Spielberg regarding the depiction of Black September terrorists as "militants," even though they murdered eleven Israelis in cold blood in an act of terror that stunned the world.

"I think the thing I'm very proud of is that [screenwriter] Tony Kushner and I and the actors did not demonize anyone in the film. We don't demonize our targets. They're individuals. They have families. Although what happened in Munich, I condemn," said Spielberg in an interview with *Time Magazine*.

The terrorists responded to Spielberg's statements, but they wanted me to clarify they didn't see the movie and based their conclusions on the depiction of *Munich* as I described it.

"We think Spielberg understands that the key is in the Israeli occupation and that no retaliation can stop the Palestinian resistance," said Senakreh. "I did not see the film and I do not need to in order to understand that all the coming generation will fight the occupation."

Adassi commented, "The Israelis don't understand what Spielberg understood, that we do not kill because we like too. We fight because we want to live and the Israeli retaliation and crimes only give us more reason to fight. It seems like Spielberg wanted to say that Israelis are breaking the international law and are pushing the Palestinians to more attacks."

During my chat with the terrorists about Hollywood, I happened to mention actor Mel Gibson, whose film, *The Passion of the Christ*, was criticized for alleged anti-Semitic imagery and overtones. The terrorists were offended by the very making of a movie depicting Jesus as a Christian leader when they say he foreshadowed Islam. But then I told the terrorists about Gibson's drunken tirade against Jews, and it seems they were willing to forgive the actor for his Christianity.

On July 28, 2006, Gibson was arrested in California for speeding and for suspicion of drunk driving. According to a police report leaked to the Internet, Gibson was abusive toward the arresting officers and remarked "F*cking Jews are responsible for all the wars in the world," asking one of them, "Are you a Jew?"

Gibson later issued two apologies through his publicist for the incident, denying being an anti-Semite.

I read to the terrorists Gibson's drunken remarks. They said they suspect Gibson's apology was to "endear himself" to the "Jews who control Hollywood."

The terrorists agreed with every word of Gibson's anti-Jewish tirade and urged the actor/director to make movies against the Jews.

"Do you really think what Gibson said is not true?" asked Adassi, speaking to a Jew. "Give me one honest and sincere person who doesn't think that this is the case. Gibson must make more films in order to explain to the Americans that not only Jews control you, they are accelerating your collapse. I tell Gibson, thank you for being conscious and honest in presenting things like they really are, but you must mobilize your audience, your people against the Jews because they are the base of all the bad and injustices in the world. Mr. Gibson, you should be strengthened to speak the truth about the Jews even when you're not drunk.

"It is not enough that Gibson says what he says, he must act in order to save your country and the whole world from the Zionist Jews. I don't mean all Jews, I don't mean you, but I'm referring to the Zionist controllers," said Senakreh.

"For the security and stability of the world, put an end to this Zionist control," Senakreh said.

◇

During my conversations with the terror leaders, it became clear a lot seemed to be generally aware how powerful American talk radio is in the U.S.

Talk radio has become one of the most important disseminators of crucial news stories Americans need to know but which wouldn't see the light of day if it were up to the mainstream media. Dinosaurs in the news world such as the *NY Times* and some top network news anchors are becoming more and more irrelevant as audiences explode on the Internet and talk radio, which have formed a nexus to bypass the mainstream media and present Americans with an alternate source of opinions and information.

Arab news media have in the past credited some U.S. policies in the Middle East to the "American conservative establishment" and talk radio, such as support for the war in Iraq and even specific measures like American pressure applied to the Israeli government to cancel the construction of a mosque in Nazareth that was going to be built in front of the Church of the Annunciation, where Christians believe Mary, the mother of Jesus, as a virgin, was visited by the Archangel Gabriel and told that she had been selected to be the mother of Jesus.

Palestinian terrorists, though, see talk radio in an entirely different, off the charts wacko way. They think American talk radio hosts are Zionist collaborators paid off to work up the masses into doing Israel's dirty work. The terrorists see my role on American radio more as informative so they are willing to talk with me. They didn't know the names of any specific American radio hosts, aside from one or two I previously mentioned to them, including one that they met.

I tried to correct the terrorists' views of talk radio and described to them very accurately the positions of some top radio hosts, including Sean Hannity, Michael Savage, Rush Limbaugh, G. Gordon Liddy, Rusty Humphries, Michael Reagan, Laura Ingraham, and Tammy Bruce, among others.

I read to the terrorists some of the hosts' on-the-air statements such as Hannity urging support for the war in Iraq, calling terrorist archenemy George Bush a "man of principle, a man of faith. ...he's got a backbone of steel and he's a real, genuine, big-time leader," and slamming Syria as a "state-sponsor of terror...it foments terror, supports terror, supports these terror organizations, and even the funding of the insurgency that is out there killing American troops."

I read quotes of Rush Limbaugh labeling anti–Iraq war protesters "Anti-American, Anti-Capitalist Marxists and Communists," and referring to the Iraq Study Group as the "Iraq Surrender Group." The group, led by former Secretary of State James Baker, recommended dialogue with Iraqi insurgents, Iran, Syria, and Israeli withdrawals from the strategic West Bank and Golan Heights.

Limbaugh stated he "wanted to puke" while listening to ISG members discussing their recommendations, asserting the "Iraq Surrender Group" members are "doing everything they can to unite the American people" in "defeat" and "surrender."

I informed them of G. Gordon Liddy's asking whether moderate Muslims existed.

Hearing enough, the terrorists called Hannity, Limbaugh, Liddy and crew "crazy racist Nazis."

Brigades chief Ala Senakreh said the hosts are "opportunistic Nazi fellows whom I am sure don't have children fighting in Iraq, who are enjoying life far from the war and from the pain the families who have children in Iraq are feeling. These are fanatic people who do not like peace. Anti-Islam racists that must be tossed in the garbage can."

Hamid accused the hosts of "serving Israel and not America. They must understand America's prosperity is because of its alliance with Muslim countries and this policy will turn Saudi Arabia, Pakistan, and other countries into enemies of America. The war the radio bastards are calling against Islam will become a harder war against your own country."

Terrorist Adassi said the radio hosts "have psychological problems," explaining the top hosts likely suffered from traumatic childhoods.

"Although you are telling me these people are successful hosts, I think they suffer from psychological complexes related to failures they had in their miserable past, maybe problems in their childhood, but they will do everything, even if it will cost the lives of millions of Americans, in order to prevent one more new failure in Iraq, because it reminds them of their failures," diagnosed Adassi.

Continued the psychoanalytical terrorist: "At the end I think these people are well paid by the Zionists; therefore, they call for more wars and feed the war against Islam. I tell them you are losing in Iraq, your allies lost in Lebanon and Gaza. Islam, the religion of Allah, will not be defeated, especially not when it has pathetic enemies like you. You damned hosts are responsible for your American soldiers who are killed daily in Iraq."

"I tell these people what is your goal? I am asking these crazy people what do you want to achieve? I ask them don't you have eyes? Don't you see your country humiliated and defeated in Iraq?" asked Adassi.

◇

For my job as a Mideast-based reporter for the popular news site *WorldNetDaily.com*, I routinely talk to terror leaders about various news events related to our neck of the woods. I garner their quotes, which usually include vicious anti-American and anti-Israeli propaganda and all kinds of wacky conspiracies. I was amazed when several times I would obtain quotes from terrorists about the day's news and then see posted on *WorldNetDaily* quotes on the same topic from television personality Rosie O'Donnell, who during the period I penned most of this book was serving as a host of ABC's *The View*. Incredibly, O'Donnell many times made almost the exact same statements as the terrorists regarding the day's news, sharing the same views as some of America's enemies on some very important topics.

One of many examples was in March 2007, when transcripts were released in which captured alleged 9/11 mastermind Khalid Sheikh Mohammed confessed to the mega-terror attacks and thirty-one other plots and attacks.

"I was responsible for the 9/11 operation from A to Z," Mohammed said in a statement. He also took credit for personally beheading *Wall Street Journal* reporter Daniel Pearl and for planning multiple other attacks since the early 1990s.

Immediately after Mohammed's confessions were released, I called the terror leaders, who unanimously explained the confessions were false and were manipulated and forced from Mohammed by a desperate Bush administration.

Abu Jihad, a West Bank leader of the Islamic Jihad terror organization, said Bush "is under a lot of pressure for victories, so I am sure as part of changing the American public opinion [Bush] needed to orchestrate this confession so he can say he is succeeding even though he is a failure."

"I am sure the Americans tortured Mohammed and forced him to say these untrue things. Isn't it strange it took three years since his arrest for the supposed confession? Intelligence agencies are known to make people say they are guilty even though they know it's not the case," Abu Jihad said.

Continued the Islamic Jihad terror leader: "With all the respect we have for al-Qaida, the story of 9/11 remains open. There are many questions about the role of Israel and the Zionists in the affair. America just wants to lie to everybody so they can put people at ease by claiming they caught the culprit."

Abu Jihad's sentiments were parroted by multiple other terrorists I interviewed on the Mohammed subject that day.

Then I read a transcript of Rosie's statements on the Mohammed affair from the day's edition of *The View*, in which the talk host suggested our government elicited a false confession from the alleged terror mastermind.

Pointing out Mohammed was arrested in March 2003, O'Donnell asked, "Why hasn't he admitted it until now?"

"They didn't allow reporters there and he hasn't had a lawyer," Rosie stated on air, insinuating Mohammed's confession was coerced with no accountability.

"I think the man has been under custody in secret CIA torture prisons and Guantanamo Bay where torture is accepted and allowed—and he finally is the guy who admits to doing *everything*," O'Donnell said. "They finally found the guy, it's not that guy bin Laden, it's this guy they've had since March 2003."

Suggesting the U.S. is looking for a scapegoat, O'Donnell said of Mohammed, "for whatever he did or didn't do, he is not the be all, end all of terrorism in America. And our government has not found the answer in this one man."

Another time, in March 2007, when Iran seized fifteen British sailors accused of violating Iranian waters, the terrorists spewed crazed theories that the affair really was orchestrated by a war-hungry Bush administration, seeking an excuse to go to war with Iran.

Lo' and behold, later in the day, I read a transcript from *The View* in which O'Donnell implied the Iranian seizure was a hoax to provide President Bush with an excuse to go to war with Tehran.

"Yes, but it's very interesting too that, you know, these guys, they went into the water by mistake right at a time when British and American, you know, they're two, they're pretty much our biggest ally and we're considering whether or not we should go into war with Iran," said good ol' Rosie.

The terrorists had never heard of O'Donnell, but I detailed her views for them very accurately. They immediately noticed how many times her statements and theories jibed almost word for word with their own stated views.

I read to the terror leaders multiple Rosie gems, like the time she argued jailed terrorists are people too and asserted the U.S. "robs them of their humanity."

"They've been treating them like animals...they have hoods over their heads, they torture them on a daily basis," she said.

On one episode of *The View,* O'Donnell said Americans shouldn't fear so-called terrorists, calling them mothers and fathers.

"Faith or fear, that's your choice," she said. "You can walk through life believing in the goodness of the world, or walk through life afraid of anyone who thinks different than you and trying to convert them to your way of thinking."

"Don't fear the terrorists. They're mothers and fathers," said O'Donnell.

The terrorists were absolutely ecstatic. At first they thought I was making up the Rosie quotes. Even after hearing unpatriotic statements from Penn and Fonda, they still couldn't believe an American would say the kinds of things Rosie uttered. It took me some time to convince the terrorists the great Rosie O'Donnell really does exist.

The one Rosie statement that won all the terrorists over beyond the others was when I told them O'Donnell raised questions on her online blog about the 9/11 attacks, implying the buildings were brought down in part to destroy documents incriminating oil giant Enron and other major corporations.

After pointing out conspiracy "factoids" regarding the World Trade Center's Building No. 7, which collapsed after the two larger "twin towers" fell, O'Donnell writes building 7 "contained offices of the FBI, Department of Defense, IRS (which contained prodigious amounts of corporate tax fraud, including Enron's), U.S. Secret Service, Securities & Exchange Commission (with more stock fraud records), and Citibank's Salomon Smith Barney, the Mayor's Office of Emergency Management and many other financial institutions consists of a listing of various records supposedly destroyed in the collapse of WTC7."

The terrorists were in love with Rosie.

"I agree with everything this O'Donnell said," boasted Adassi. "Regarding September 11, there is no way the American intelligence and administration was not aware of what was going to happen that day. How come the Jews and Israelis disappeared from the buildings? Was it by miracle? They knew that an attack would take place. This meant that Zionist elements and the leading elements of the administration who are aligned with economic companies and interests, like Bush and Cheney's companies of oil, were very interested that the attack would succeed in order to start their campaign for the oil of Iran and Afghanistan."

Jews did not "disappear" from the buildings.

Brigades chieftain Senakreh commented, "Many people have been saying this since the first moment it happened. Of course when it comes from persons like O'Donnell it takes a more serious significance. I guess she knows what she is saying."

The terrorists went on to invite Rosie to come live among them in the West Bank and Gaza Strip, where they said they would ensure she is treated "like a queen."

"We welcome Rosie O'Donnell to live among us and to get to know the truth from being here, like many American peace activists are doing. It would be a great honor for us if she comes and live with us," said Senakreh.

"I think that she is a mother and she knows what she is saying. We are not in love with killing, we like peace, we are human beings, it is the occupation that obliges us to do what we do," Senakreh said.

Adassi agreed and also extended an invitation to Rosie. "She will be most welcomed if she decides to visit us or live here and to get to know what your allies, the Israelis, are doing against our people. We thank her for telling and presenting the truth."

Then I broke the terrorists' hearts and informed them their beloved Rosie is also a big outspoken lesbian who proudly lives with her female partner.

The terrorists said Rosie can only move to Gaza if she ceased her "Satanic ways" and agreed to abide by the rules of Islam regarding sexual relations.

"Let her still come," said Adassi. "We will teach her the right ways. She is already on the right path."

CHAPTER SIX

HOW YOU FUND TERRORISM

MARCH 1, 1973. Eight members of the Black September terrorist organization, part of Yasser Arafat's Fatah faction of the Palestine Liberation Organization, stormed the Saudi Arabian embassy in Khartoum, taking U.S. Ambassador Cleo Noel and the U.S. embassy's Charge d'Affaires George Curtis Moore and several others hostage.

The siege occurred during a publicly announced diplomatic reception honoring a local U.S. diplomat, leading many to speculate the Americans were the main targets.

One day later, on March 2, 1973, our two diplomats, Noel and Moore, were machine-gunned to death by Arafat's men—it turns out on Arafat's direct orders.

Since the late 1990s, James J. Welsh, the National Security Agency's Palestinian analyst at the time of the murder of our diplomats, has been telling anyone who will listen the NSA had tapes of Arafat ordering the executions of the American men.

Welsh was a primary analyst and interpreter of Arafat's communications for the NSA. He said in 1973, just before the embassy was taken hostage, he intercepted a transmission directly from Arafat involving an imminent operation in Khartoum. Welsh's NSA superiors were alerted. The next day, the Black September operation took place.

There was immediate information Arafat personally sent the order for the execution of the American diplomats to the terrorists via a radio broadcast in which he uttered: "Why are you waiting? The people's blood in the Cold River cries for vengeance."

"Cold River" was reportedly known to the American intelligence apparatus as the code word for executing the captives. Supposed NSA recordings of that call have disappeared.

In 1985 and 1986, Congress requested then–Attorney General Ed Meese to investigate Arafat's complicity in the murders of the diplomats. But Meese didn't come up with much.

On February 12, 1986, some forty-seven U.S. senators, including Al Gore, petitioned Meese "to assign the highest priority to completing this review, and to issue an indictment of Yasser Arafat if the evidence so warrants."

But no evidence was produced by the NSA, the Central Intelligence Agency, or the State Department. That would have ruined Arafat's glowing image as a statesmen who wants peace with Israel.

For years U.S. policy deceptively deemed Arafat "moderate." With enormous American assistance, Arafat, who pioneered many of the tactics used today by terrorists worldwide, established a Palestinian fiefdom in the Gaza Strip and West Bank. He was provided billions in U.S. and international aid. He shook hands in 1993 at a ceremony on the White House lawn with Israel's prime minister and America's president. Arafat went on to win himself a Nobel Peace Prize. He became the foreign leader to most frequent the Clinton White House.

That same Arafat ordered the murder of our men. Only the public didn't know it.

Welsh watched in horror as our government built up the murderer of our two diplomats. He petitioned multiple news agencies to report his story but was widely ignored by the mainstream media in spite of the sensationalism of the accusations—the NSA analyst in charge of Arafat's transmissions claimed the government had evidence the PLO leader ordered the brutal killings of Noel and Moore.

In 2000, Arafat turned down U.S.-mediated talks offering a Palestinian state in the West Bank, Gaza, and eastern Jerusalem, and instead returned to Israel to launch a terrorist war that killed thousands of Israelis and Palestinians and several Americans. The father of modern terrorism died of mysterious causes in a Paris hospital in 2004.

Then, in 2006, something incredible happened. The U.S. government admitted it possessed evidence for thirty-three years that Arafat ordered the killings of Noel and Moore.

A declassified State Department document from 1973 outlining U.S. findings into the Khartoum operation states:

> The Khartoum operation was planned and carried out with the full knowledge and personal approval of Yasir (sic) Arafat, Chairman of the Palestine Liberation Organization, and the head of Fatah. Fatah representatives based in Khartoum participated in the attack, using a Fatah vehicle to transport the terrorists to the Saudi Arabian Embassy.

This was one of the most monumental admissions in the history of the American government. The U.S. knew Arafat killed our diplomats but went to great lengths to hide that information, instead building up this mass murderer as some sort of peace lover, providing him with enormous sums of money, weapons, legitimacy, and other kinds of aid.

Now, in the midst of America's war on terror, it's happening all over again but in even more direct ways. The U.S. is funding, arming and fueling terrorists with your hard-earned tax dollars.

<><

"I just shot at a school bus," said the breathless voice on the other line. I could hear the man was running.

"I am taking credit for the attack in the memory of Abu Ammar [Arafat] in the name of the Al Aqsa Martyrs Brigades. I used my American assault rifle," said the man, Abu Yousuf, an officer of Force 17, the presidential guard unit of Palestinian Authority President Mahmoud Abbas's Fatah organization.

It was a hot summer day on June 19, 2006. I was relaxing at a hotel spa in the Dead Sea, the lowest point on earth and one of my favorite places in the world. I spend as much free time as I can at the sea. I had just finished luxuriating in a slightly heated indoor sulfur pool and was on my way to a generous buffet lunch before heading into the soothing sea for the rest of the day. I could spend hours bathing in the Dead Sea, even though some say more than one hour in the extremely salty waters can be too much. But ruining the vacation mood, Abu Yousuf called me to boast he just shot up a bus it turned out was transporting schoolgirls.

"I think the attack was successful. Can you find out?" asked Abu Yousuf, before he abruptly ended the call.

Abu Yousuf, a man trained, armed, and funded by the U.S., just used a brand new high powered assault rifle paid for by you and me and delivered by the U.S. to snipe at a busload of school girls.

I had been introduced to Abu Yousuf several months earlier during a series of articles I wrote about Fatah's militias, which regularly receive American training, funding, and weapons. I was stunned to learn many members of the Fatah militias are openly also members of the Al Aqsa Martyrs Brigades, the declared military wing of Fatah, which is classified by the U.S. State Department as a terror organization. The U.S. regularly provides weapons and funding to Fatah militias.

Together with the Islamic Jihad terror group, the Brigades took responsibility for every suicide bombing in Israel in 2005, 2006, and 2007. It has carried out scores of deadly shootings and rocket attacks. It's one of the most active, dangerous terror organizations in the world today.

Fatah was the party of Arafat. U.S. policy largely calls Fatah "moderate," and claims its leader, Abbas, wants peace.

Ridiculously, many Americans think when it comes to the Palestinians, Fatah is good and Hamas is bad. But the major difference between the two is Hamas only attacks Israelis whereas Fatah attacks Israelis and conducts "peace negotiations" at the same time.

Fatah's television networks regularly urge suicide bombings. Fatah's Al Aqsa Martyrs Brigades terror group has since 2005 been responsible for more terrorism than Hamas. Fatah leader Abbas wrote a thesis denying the Holocaust. He was one of the main deputies of Arafat, one of the most prominent terrorists of his time. Claiming Abbas is moderate would be like instilling in 1946 as the new leader of Germany Adolph Hitler's main deputy who carried out all of Hitler's policies, and then claiming said deputy was miraculously now pro-Jew.

It took no investigative reporting whatsoever on my part to discover members of U.S.-backed, trained, and armed Fatah militias are also members of the Al Aqsa Martyrs Brigades terror group. I simply went around the West Bank and asked Fatah militia members, who walk around with American-provided high-power assault rifles, whether they are also in the Brigades. A lot said yes. I then confirmed the names with Brigades leaders. Also multiple Fatah officials are members of the Brigades.

"During our official service and during our job hours we are soldiers for Fatah. What we do in our free time is our business," Abu Yousuf told me upon our first conversation. "Of course as members of Fatah, some of us are members in the Brigades and we take part in the defense and protection of our people and in the fight against the Israeli occupation."

By fight against Israeli occupation, Abu Yousuf means sending suicide bombers into restaurants and nightclubs.

Meet Abu Yousuf. He's a thirty-four-year-old resident of the West Bank city of Ramallah. He served as an officer of the Preventative Security Services, a kind of police unit in the Gaza Strip and West Bank. He's currently an officer of Force 17, Abbas's presidential guard units, which protect Fatah officials and sometimes serve as police officers.

Yousuf previously carried out scores of terror attacks, including several shootings against Israeli civilians, attacks against Israeli forces operating in Ramallah and a shooting attack in northern Samaria in December 2000 that killed Benyamin Kahane, leader of the ultranationalist Kahane Chai organization and son of the group's founder, Meir Kahane, who was also assassinated.

Like many Force 17 members, Yousuf is openly a member of the Al Aqsa Martyrs Brigades. His specific Brigades cell has sent several suicide bombers into Israel.

As part of the Preventative Security Services, Abu Yousuf received training at a base in the West Bank town of Jericho run by a U.S. security team. There, our American tax dollars paid for this terrorist to learn from Americans how to shoot, collect intelligence, and conduct guerilla-style raids.

Abu Yousuf described to me his American training:

> I myself received American trainings in Jericho. Together with my Preventative comrades, I received trainings in intelligence methods and military trainings. In the intelligence part, we learned collection of information regarding suspected persons, how to follow suspected guys, how to infiltrate organizations and penetrate cells of groups that we were working on and how to prevent attacks and to steal in places.
>
> On the military level, we received trainings on the use of weapons, all kind of weapons and explosives. We received sniping trainings, work of special units especially as part as what they call the fight against terror. We learned how to put siege, how to break into places where our enemies closed themselves in, how to oppress protest movements, demonstrations and other activities of opposition.

Abu Yousuf told me he used his American training to kill the Israelis:

> We sniped at Israeli settlers and soldiers. We broke into settlements and Israeli army bases and posts. We collected information on the movements of soldiers and settlers. We collected information about the best timing to infiltrate our bombers inside Israel. We used weapons and we produced explosives, and of course the trainings we received from the Americans and the Europeans were a great help to the resistance.

Yousuf said he only shot at soldiers and "settlers;" settlers meaning Jewish residents of the West Bank. But actually he also shot at Israelis who live in central Israel but who were driving through the West Bank and his group sent suicide bombers to Jerusalem and Tel Aviv.

Continued Abu Yousuf: "All the methods and techniques that we studied in these trainings, we applied them against the Israelis. We also learned to discover agents that Israel tried to plant in our cells."

"I do not think that the operations of the Palestinian resistance would have been so successful and would have killed more than one thousand Israelis since 2000 and defeated the Israelis in Gaza without these [American] trainings.

"I am not saying this in order to irritate the Americans or the Israelis and not in order to create provocations. I'm just telling you the truth. We applied against Israel all that we learned from you Americans."

Indeed, Abu Yousuf's Al Aqsa Martyrs Brigades was one of the most active groups during the Palestinian *intifada*, or terror war initiated by Yasser Arafat after Bill Clinton–mediated peace talks broke down in the summer of 2000. As of this writing, 1,029 Israelis and over twenty Americans were killed during the *intifada*, whose fighters Abu Yousuf said utilized U.S. training.

Abu Yousuf said he is up for possible future American training as a member of Force 17. And in May 2006, he was hand-delivered a brand new American assault rifle paid for by you and me.

It was widely reported that in May 2006 America sent to Fatah militias a cache of three thousand M-16 assault rifles and over one million rounds of ammunition. At first, a shipment of only three hundred was admitted to. Israeli Prime Minister Ehud Olmert announced he had approved the shipment of U.S. weapons and ammunition to Fatah, explaining the transfer was meant to bolster Abbas's Fatah organization in clashes against the Hamas terror group.

According to Israeli and Palestinian officials involved in the May assault rifles transfer, the American arms shipment originated in Jordan and needed Israel's approval for transport. The Israeli Defense Forces escorted the American shipment to the West Bank town of Ramallah, where the weapons were delivered to the main Fatah compound, known as the Muqata. A second convoy delivered weapons to the Gaza Strip.

The Muqata was once the infamous home of Arafat. After the Benyamin Kahane murder, Arafat extended Abu Yousuf refuge to live in the Muqata, where he still sleeps from time to time to this day because he knows Israel is reluctant to raid the compound. Parts of the Muqata were previously bombed, but a lot of the structure is still standing. Yousuf resides in the Muqata during periods of tension with Israel. Other terrorists from the Al Aqsa Martyrs Brigades also live in the Muqata when they need to. All this is no secret. Israeli security officials know all about it. There's no excuse for American security coordinators in the West Bank to be in the dark about the fact American weapons are being delivered to a compound in which known terrorists reside.

A few days after the American weapons were received in the Muqata, there was an unusually high number of shootings against Israeli motorists in and near the West Bank carried out by Al Aqsa Brigades terrorists.

Sources close to the Brigades told me the new American assault rifles were used in three separate anti-Israel shooting attacks carried out within weeks of the weapons shipment. One attack killed a thirty-five-year-old Israeli Arab on a major West Bank highway on the outskirts of Jerusalem. Israeli security officials say the shooters likely mistook the victim for a Jew. The second attack occurred June 13 on the same highway, lightly wounding an Israeli.

The third attack was Abu Yousuf's bus shooting against Israeli school girls. Turned out Abu Yousuf's cowardly shooting failed. The bus, traveling in the northern West Bank, was armored. Three schoolgirls were lightly injured. Security officials said if the bus had not been armored, the injuries would have been more serious.

Make no mistake about it. America provided Abu Yousuf the tools to carry out his attack.

"It is no coincidence that as soon as these American weapons arrived, we were able to carry out these accurate shootings," Abu Yousuf said.

Abu Yousuf told me the U.S. sent weapons to Fatah "for its own political purposes and as part of a conspiracy to generate a civil war between us and Hamas. We are not concerned with the reasons. The weapons will not be used against our brothers, only [against] Israelis."

U.S.-Trained Terror Group

Nablus, a northern West Bank city saturated in terror, is the main stronghold and breeding grounds for the Al Aqsa Martyrs Brigades. The entire senior leadership of the Brigades in Nablus, every single one of them, is U.S.-trained. The majority of the Brigades serve in various Fatah militias.

The leader of the Brigades in Nablus, Ala Senakreh, was trained by the U.S. in Jericho. He also serves in the Palestinian Preventative Security Services. In other words, a U.S.-trained police officer charged with stopping terrorism in Nablus is also the known head of the city's terror group. Something smells a little wrong here.

I once met Ala Senakreh in Nablus and he told me he had used his U.S.-provided rifle less than twenty-four hours earlier to "shoot at the Israelis." Senakreh's cell has orchestrated at least four suicide bombings inside Israel.

The deputy commander of the Brigades in Nablus, Nasser Abu Aziz, is also U.S.-trained. He received training in Italy, as well. He's personally killed at least four Israelis in shooting attacks, and together with Senakreh, aided in planning several suicide bombings.

Zacharias Zubeidi, well-known leader of the Brigades in Jenin—the city where most Palestinian suicide bombers originate—was trained by our government in Jericho.

The theme goes on.

Israel regularly arrests U.S.-trained Fatah members wielding American weapons who are wanted for terror attacks and who used their American training to carry out their operations. In the months leading up to this book's publication, dozens of U.S.-trained terrorists were arrested in Ramallah alone.

Once, a senior terrorist working for Fatah was caught by me transporting weapons just delivered by the U.S. On February 1, 2007, Hamas ambushed a Fatah Force 17 convoy the terror group claimed was transporting American weapons delivered the night before to a Fatah compound in the Gaza Strip. A battle raged between Hamas gunmen and Force 17 guards accompanying the convoy. Four Force 17 officers were killed. The Islamic Jihad terror group told me among those killed serving with Force 17 was Nidal Tlaa, the chief commander of Islamic Jihad's so-called military wing. He was wearing his Force 17 uniform when he was shot. So the overall leader of Islamic Jihad's terror wing in Gaza also doubled as a U.S.-funded Fatah officer whose rank was so high he was trusted with transporting American weapons shipments.

And yet America keeps sending Fatah weapons and keeps training its militias. Better to deal with the bad guy you know, perhaps the thinking goes. The three thousand assault rifles reported in May 2006 were just the tip of the iceberg. There are weapons shipments to Fatah all the time that go unreported. I am in touch with officials on both the Israeli and Palestinian sides who coordinate the arrival and delivery of the American weapons. I am alerted to a lot of the U.S. weapons shipments to Fatah, like a shipment in January 2007 of over seven thousand assault rifles and more than one million rounds of ammunition purportedly to bolster Fatah against rival Hamas factions while the two were engaged in firefights. A shipment of three thousand assault rifles arrived in July 2007.

I am not sure Congress knows the extent of American arms regularly flooded to Fatah. We're talking over $200 million worth of weapons in 2006 alone in addition to all the publicly declared financial support of the Palestinians, which has amounted to nearly $1.8 billion in direct aid to the PA and nongovernmental organizations operating in the Palestinian territories since 1994 and more than $1.1 billion to the United Nations organizations that work with the Palestinians.

After the January shipment of seven thousand American assault rifles arrived, I asked Abu Yousuf what his group would do with the arms.

"The first place of these U.S. weapons will be to defend the Palestinian national project, which is reflected by the foundation of the Palestinian Authority. If Hamas or any other group under the influence of Iran and Syria wants to make a *coup d'etat* against our institution, these weapons are there to defend the PA," Abu Yousuf told me days after a new cache arrived.

But the Fatah militant said the new American weapons shipments may also be used to target Israelis.

"If we find ourselves manipulated by Israel, we cannot guarantee members of the Al Aqsa Martyrs Brigades and Force 17 will not use these weapons against Israel. Our goal is to change the occupation," said Abu Yousuf.

"It's unnatural to think these American weapons won't be used against the Israelis," he said.

Abu Yousuf said the American weapons shipments may be shared with other Palestinian terror groups. He said that during large confrontations with Israel, such as the Jewish state's 2002 anti-terror raid in Jenin, Fatah distributed weapons to Hamas and Islamic Jihad.

"We don't look where this piece or that piece of weapon came from when fighting the Israelis," Abu Yousuf said.

There was a brief period I thought Congress understood the U.S. was supporting terrorism and almost blocked aid to Fatah militias. During the fiasco Secretary of State Condoleezza Rice conceded she cannot guarantee American money and weapons sent to Fatah won't "get into the wrong hands."

The Bush administration in January pledged $86.4 million to strengthen the Fatah forces, including Force 17. The funds would be used to implement a security plan devised by Lt. Gen. Keith Dayton, the American security coordinator in the region. Dayton's plan called for some $14.5 million for "basic and advanced training" of Fatah fighters, $23 million for equipment, $2.9 million to upgrade Force 17 facilities and $3 million to provide "capacity building and technical assistance" to the office of Dahlan, Fatah's strongman in Gaza.

But after a series of articles, including several of mine, outlining how Fatah consists of terrorists, Congress blocked the aid pending a clarification from Rice.

During a Congressional hearing in March 2007, Rice conceded she can't account for where the aid will go. She said she would request less money.

"I will request less money, precisely because some of the money that I would have requested I did not think I could fully account for. I hope that is a sign for you that we take very seriously our responsibilities. I have no interest in having to come here one day and say, 'you know this funding did not end up in the right place.' I will do my very best," she told Congress.

Lawmakers caught the State Department red-handed. The U.S. was about to send money Rice admitted may get into the wrong hands. But then Rice simply asked for $59 million instead of $86.5 million to fund the same terror-saturated Fatah militias. And Congress bought it. They unfroze the aid, but put on one new qualification stipulating the money must not be used to purchase weapons. The State Department is free to send more weapons to Fatah, which they will, just not from this particular aid package, which instead will only train terrorists but not arm them and anyway is likely only a fraction of the funding to Fatah that Congress knows about.

Congress, by the way, didn't express much worry Fatah fighters are also terrorists. Instead, they were mostly worried Hamas might get their hands on the weapons. Congress naively thinks Fatah is moderate. In the end they allowed the money after assurances the funds won't train Hamas.

Well, I can assure Congress the $59 million in American funds they approved in 2007 will indeed train Hamas since Hamas is very well placed within U.S.-funded Fatah forces, according to Israeli security officials, Fatah security officials, and the Hamas terrorists themselves.

Israeli security officials say Hamas has infiltrated all major Fatah security forces, including Force 17.

A top Palestinian intelligence official speaking to me in Ramallah admitted, "We are leading a large number of investigations and some of the results prove that such an infiltration by Hamas (of Fatah's security and intelligence forces) exists."

The official oversees intelligence for Fatah's police forces in the West Bank and Gaza Strip.

"I can say that in some cases we diagnosed a deep infiltration to high posts in some Fatah security services," said the Palestinian intelligence officer. "In some cases we believe there are officers that are exposed to very sensitive information."

He said that since the Bush administration announced it was providing Abbas's forces with additional funds, Fatah intelligence officials at the direction of American security coordinators have been attempting to expel Hamas infiltrators. He said in one month alone "dozens" of members of Hamas, the Popular Resistance Committees, and Islamic Jihad were found operating in the Fatah forces.

The Committees regularly carries out terror attacks, including rocket launchings, shootings and kidnappings. It is accused of a 2003 bombing of a U.S. convoy in Gaza in which three American contractors were killed.

Muhammad Abdel-El, spokesman for the Committees, told me Fatah's attempts to discover militants from his group "have not even scratched the surface of our infiltration."

"We are very well-placed within Fatah's units and their little investigations made no difference," he said.

He said the Committees will obtain the U.S. aid and any American arms given to Fatah: "In all the security services, including in Force 17, there are activists affiliated with all the Palestinian groups, including ours, and Hamas," he said. "We vow that this American money will be used against the occupation and the Zionist enemy."

Similarly, Abu Oubaida, a spokesman for Hamas, told me his terror group will obtain any U.S. aid or weapons transferred to Fatah militias.

"I am sure that like in the past, this $59 million from America will find its way to the Hamas resistance via the honorable persons in the Fatah security organizations, including in Force 17. I can confirm 100 percent that this money will find its way to Hamas," said Abu Oubaida.

Even if Fatah wasn't infiltrated by Hamas, which they are, logic dictates if you arm one terror group against another, it will create an arms race with the competing group. Indeed that is exactly what happened with Hamas, which fairly easily obtained enormous quantities of weaponry from its Iranian backers.

"The more the Americans give Abu Mazen [Abbas] weapons, the more we will have in the future weapons to use against the

Israelis, because it incites the different organizations to intensify their own supply of weapons," Hamas's Abu Abdullah told me.

Rendering Fatah's U.S.-backed investigation to oust Hamas from its midst completely farcical, in April 2007, Hamas and Fatah approved a plan to incorporate Hamas militias and terror cells into a unified security force under the authority of Abbas. According to the plan, Hamas's so-called military wing, responsible for scores of anti-Israel terror attacks, would have been allowed to continue operating under the aegis of the PA's Interior Ministry. The plan calls for all armed organizations, including the Al Aqsa Martyrs Brigades terror group, to maintain a single operations center under the command of Abbas.

The terror unity agreement was forged just days after Congress approved the $59 million in aid to Fatah! Of course, it never came about; Hamas and Fatah basically waged war against each other.

But I've witnessed things even more ridiculous. In one of the most absurd moments I experienced as a reporter in Israel, days after the January 2007 shipment of seven thousand American assault rifles purportedly to arm Abbas's Fatah militias against Hamas, Abbas gave a public speech in Ramallah in front of hundreds of Palestinians and the international news media in which he urged Palestinians to use their assault rifles against Israel instead of Hamas.

"Shooting at your brother is forbidden. Raising rifles against the occupation is our legitimate right, but raising guns against each other is forbidden. We should put our internal fighting aside and raise our rifles only against the Israeli occupation," said Abbas during the speech, which I attended and which was part of a ceremony commemorating the forty-second anniversary of the founding of his Fatah party.

Abbas then used Quranic verses to claim Jews are corrupting the world.

"The sons of Israel are mentioned as those who are corrupting humanity on earth," Abbas said during a portion of his speech in which he criticized recent Israeli anti-terror raids in the northern West Bank.

Incredibly, Abbas's anti-Semitic remarks and his call to arms against the Jewish state were not quoted in scores of English-language articles reporting on the speech or by most major Israeli dailies, which featured pieces on their websites about the Fatah commemoration ceremonies.

Most of the articles, written by reporters in attendance, claimed Abbas gave a talk about making peace with Israel. Some of the articles deliberated cut out Abbas's anti-Israel remarks. For example, a widely circulated *Associated Press* article, titled "Abbas calls for respect at Fatah rally," stated Abbas used his speech to call for rival factions to respect each other.

The AP quotes Abbas stating, "Shooting at your brother is forbidden," but the article stops short of quoting the rest of Abbas's sentence in which he recommends Palestinians use their weapons against Israel. The AP article was featured on such top websites as *WashingtonPost.com* and *CBSNews.com*. Articles by other news agencies and local Israeli papers also failed to quote Abbas's anti-Israel and anti-Semitic remarks.

Just as during the days of Arafat, the cover up of Abbas and his Fatah terror organization is so extensive Abbas can give a speech in front of the international media about raising rifles against Israel and no one even reports about it.

Hamas Hijacks CIA Documents

"The Gaza Strip has fallen. It's now Hamas land. We have lost," Chief Palestinian Negotiator Saeb Erekat yelled into his cell phone, speaking to me from Ramallah in June 2007.

Two days earlier, the Hamas terror group had launched a stunning coup in Gaza, taking complete control of the territory and overrunning all U.S.-backed Fatah security compounds and positions there, including Fatah's major Ansar complex—where massive quantities of American-provided weapons were delivered and stored—and Abbas's presidential guard complex.

Hamas was elected to power in 2006 and for the first few months of the terror group's rule, it shared a government with Abbas's Fatah party. But the Hamas leadership knew they were much stronger than Fatah in Gaza, so they acted as all violent gangs do to assume leadership—they staged a bloody uprising and seized control.

In a matter of a few days in June 2007, Hamas completely took over the Gaza Strip. In a spectacular display broadcast by the international media, Hamas overran Fatah security buildings and compounds in which U.S. security officials previously maintained a regular presence, coordinating security and weapons delivery and providing training to Abbas's militias.

When Hamas hijacked the Fatah buildings, they also obtained enormous quantities of U.S. weapons. Hamas's Al Aqsa Television immediately broadcast footage of Hamas gunmen brandishing what it said were American assault rifles, rocket-propelled grenades, rocket launchers and ammunition the U.S. reportedly provided to Fatah.

Members of Hamas's so-called military wing provided me with a preliminary list of U.S. weaponry and equipment they claimed they obtained, including dozens of mounted machine guns; approximately 7,400 American M-16 assault rifles; about 800,000 rounds of bullets; eighteen armored personnel carriers; seven armored military jeeps; "tens" of armored civilian cars, including pickup trucks and magnums; eight massive trucks equipped with water cannons for dispersing protests; and fourteen military-sized bulldozers.

Hamas members said the list didn't include what they said were large quantities of U.S.-provided rocket propelled grenades, grenade launchers, explosives, and military equipment, such as boots and tents.

Abu Abdullah, a senior member of Hamas's "military wing," said his group estimates it obtained at least $400 million worth of American weapons and equipment. While I couldn't verify that number, the average cost of an M-16 in Gaza during the time Hamas took over was $16,911, and the average cost of a bullet was $12.07, meaning the cost in Gaza of U.S. assault rifles and bullets Hamas claims to have obtained amount to over $137 million.

Not only did Hamas hijack our weaponry, it also claims to have obtained important CIA files, including documents that supposedly outline American intelligence networks in the Middle East. The CIA files were apparently also obtained by the Popular Resistance Committees, which was accused of bombing a U.S.

convoy in 2003. The Committees fought alongside Hamas during the Gaza coup.

Hamas and Popular Resistance Committees leaders told me they seized the purported CIA files upon taking over Gaza City's Fatah compounds, particularly the Preventative Security Services building and a U.S.-backed intelligence compound. They said prior to Hamas's advances, Fatah officials attempted to destroy the CIA documents but only succeeded in eliminating some.

"The CIA files we seized, which include documents, CDs, taped conversations, and videos, are more important than all the American weapons we obtained in the last days as we took over the traitor Fatah's positions," said Committees spokesman Abdel-El.

Hamas's Abu Abdullah said, "The files are crucial for our fight against the Zionists and anyone who collaborates with them, including the Americans."

Abdullah said the hijacked CIA documents contained "information about the collaboration between Fatah and the Israeli and American security organizations; CIA methods on how to prevent attacks, chase and follow after cells of Hamas and the Committees; plans about Fatah assassinations of members of Hamas and other organizations; and American studies on the security situation in Gaza."

Abdullah claimed the documents also detailed CIA networks in other Arab countries and "how to help beat Islamic allies of Hamas in other Arab countries, including Egypt and Jordan."

"We will use these documents and make portions public to prove the collaboration between America and traitor Arab countries," Abdullah said.

Abdel-El boasted he found his name mentioned four times in the CIA documents on his group.

"I am amazed by the material and the context of the documents," he said.

The brilliant U.S. plan to arm Fatah against Hamas couldn't have blown up in our faces any more than it did with Hamas's takeover of Gaza. Did we learn from our mistakes and stop funding, arming, training, and coordinating intelligence with terror thugs? Of course not. The first thing the U.S. and international community did after Hamas's Gaza seizure was pledge more aid and send more weapons to Abbas in the West Bank to ensure against a Hamas takeover there.

Abu Abdullah told me, "Like the American weapons in Gaza we told you will come to Hamas, also the weapons and aid the Americans are giving to Abu Mazen [Abbas] as part of their conspiracy against us in the West Bank will find its way to the Palestinian resistance and Hamas."

Death of American Teenager "Gift from Allah"

It was a hot day in April 2006. Jews worldwide were celebrating the fifth day of the Passover holiday, one of the holiest festivals on the Jewish calendar. I was studying the laws of Passover with a rabbi in Tel Aviv when my pager beeped with the one message I most dread—"Alert, suicide bombing." The Israeli government sends regular text message alerts to accredited reporters in Israel. I was informed the bombing took place just a few blocks from where I was at the time, so I rushed to the scene.

The blast ripped through a *falafel* restaurant outside Tel Aviv's old central bus station, killing nine and wounding dozens. By the time I arrived, ambulances had already rushed the dead and wounded from the scene. A religious Jewish group of heroes called ZAKA, a Hebrew acronym for Identifying Victims of Disaster, were sorting through the rubble for severed body parts. Jewish law considers all body parts sacred and dictates severed limbs and flesh must be buried. I saw a bloody finger and part of a foot being carefully wrapped in plastic, causing me to nearly vomit.

Then I was told there was an American victim in the attack, a teenager named Daniel Wultz, who was rushed to a nearby hospital with severe injuries. He had been dining with his father, Tuly Wultz, who was also badly injured in the blast. The Wultzes are residents of Weston, Florida. They were on Passover vacation in Israel.

Islamic Jihad and Fatah's Al Aqsa Brigades claimed responsibility for the bombing. The cell of the Brigades that directed the attack was located in Nablus, and happens to be one of the groups I am closest to. According to Brigades sources, the entire bombing operation—from the planning to the recruitment of the suicide bomber—was carried out by Fatah's Brigades. Islamic Jihad's only participation was to provide the explosive belt so they could take part in the joyous act of killing Jews.

The very crew who sent the bomber into Israel to gravely injure Daniel Wultz consisted of none other than U.S.-trained Brigades leaders who walk around with American-provided assault rifles.

Wultz, an avid basketball player, lost his spleen and a kidney in the attack. Doctors amputated one of his legs and fought to save his other leg, which was suffering from severely reduced blood flow. The sixteen-year-old was comatose.

His story generated extensive U.S. media coverage and had prompted a flurry of e-mails and messages across the Internet asking people worldwide to pray for the young terror victim.

At one very emotional point, seven days after the bombing, things momentarily looked good for Daniel. Incredibly, he opened his eyes and emerged briefly from his coma after his hometown rabbi, who flew to Israel to be with the family, wrapped his arm in scripture.

The rabbi, Yisroel Spalter of the Chabad Lubavitch Jewish outreach movement, described the moment he put *tefillin*, or Jewish prayer phylacteries containing Torah verses, on Wultz:

> I started to put the tefillin on his hand and right before our very eyes Daniel opened his eyes and stared at us despite his comatose state. Maybe it was just a reflex, maybe not, but the fact that it happened precisely when the tefillin were placed on his hand shocked us all. Even the doctors were surprised.
>
> The family members who were present could not hold back their tears and were full of emotions. I cannot describe to you the electricity that flowed through the room then. It was one of the most moving and emotional experiences I ever witnessed.

Tefillin have been directly connected to war and terrorism.

A verse in Deuteronomy states, "Then all the people of the earth shall see that the name of God is proclaimed over you and they will fear you."

The Talmud explains the biblical verse is referring to the donning of *tefillin*, which contains the name of G-d.

In response to the verse, Rabbi Menachem Mendel Schneerson, the revered leader of the heroic Chabad Lubavitch movement, promoted a *tefillin* campaign in Israel and around the world following the 1967 Six Day War, in which the Jewish state was attacked by several Arab countries.

Rabbi Spalter the next day put *tefillin* on Wultz, who soon after opened his eyes again and for the first time began showing signs of communication to his doctors, including blinking his eyes in response to questions.

But it wasn't meant to be. Daniel Wultz passed away on Sunday, May 14.

What the terrorists thought of Wultz was important to me because I saw a lot of myself in him. We are both Orthodox Jewish American citizens. Like me, Wultz attended modern religious Jewish schooling. Like me, Wultz came from a Chabad Lubavitch household. The terrorists are nice to me because they want publicity and they want to show the world they have nothing against Jews, only "Israeli occupiers," but occasions like the attacking of Wultz brought out my terror friends' true faces.

I informed the terrorists of Wultz's death. American-trained Nasser Abu Aziz, deputy commander of the Brigades in Nablus and the West Bank, called Wultz's passing a "gift from Allah." Abu Aziz's cell directed the bombing that killed Wultz.

"We wish this young dog will go directly with no transit to hell," Abu Aziz said.

"[Wultz] was part of the American support machine that helps our enemy. All these young American Jews come here to support the occupation, they build and live in the settlements...I imagine him as one of these Nazis who live here [in the settlements.] There is no difference between him and them."

I explained to Abu Aziz that Wultz was only visiting Israel, but he said he was still happy the American died.

"I say to the Americans if you will not change then we wish you more Daniel Wultzes and more pain and sorrow because it seems that this is the only thing you deserve."

Abu Aziz went on to pledge more suicide bombings inside Israel. "We will hit whenever we will think it is suitable and do not expect that I give details but we can hit everywhere," he said.

Our money helped pay for the death of Wultz and for so many others.

<>

American support to terrorism isn't limited to the funding of militias. We also pay for schools that serve as terror training zones; chemistry labs used to make explosive suicide belts; even streets in terror sanctuaries named after notorious American enemies.

The United States Agency for International Development (USAID) in 2006 provided $140,000 to the Hamas-run Islamic University in the Gaza Strip.

State Department spokesman Sean McCormack said U.S. officials concluded after a review the Islamic University of Gaza doesn't support terror activities, which is laughable.

Hamas's Abu Abdullah told me Islamic University is regularly used by Hamas to support "resistance activities."

"It is no secret that we utilize all tools at our disposal, including our fighters at Islamic University in preparations to fight the Zionists," said Abu Abdullah.

Islamic University was founded by Hamas spiritual leader Ahmed Yassin, who was assassinated by Israel in 2004.

According to Israeli and Palestinian intelligence officials, Islamic University's main campus in Gaza City has been used by Hamas's military wing to recruit terrorists and suicide bombers. The University's chemistry labs were used to manufacture and improve explosives for Hamas-affiliated militias.

Officials from Abbas's Fatah party in March 2006 claimed they captured seven Iranian military trainers—including a general of the Iranian Revolutionary Guards—inside Gaza City's Islamic University, which they said was being utilized as a Hamas military training ground.

The Fatah officials said they also found nearly one thousand Qassam rockets and equipment to manufacture the rockets inside the University. They previously suspected kidnapped Israeli soldier Gilad Shalit was being held for a time on the University grounds.

Popular Resistance Committees outspoken spokesman Muhammad Abdel-El told me Islamic University is "extremely important" for recruitment of militants. He said several members of his group study chemistry at the University to aid in the manufacture of explosives and suicide belts.

Also since September 2004, USAID has reportedly provided $4 million of our money to Arkan, a Palestinian program that funds law schools at several universities in the West Bank and Gaza Strip, including Al-Najah University.

Israeli security officials say Al-Najah University is one of the most important recruitment grounds for West Bank terror organizations. The Israeli Defense Forces a number of times raided the college and arrested terror suspects. At least fifteen Palestinians who carried out suicide bombings the past six years attended the school.

One senior leader of the Al Aqsa Martyrs Brigades told me many Brigades leaders study at the University, which he described as a "recruitment center for *jihad*." The senior leader said he himself is studying sports education.

A leader of the Islamic Jihad terror organization said he is studying chemistry at Al Najah to enhance his terror group's bomb-making capabilities. He said others in the chemistry department manufacture explosives for Palestinian groups.

Oh, by the way, according to the U.S. Foreign Operations Bill of 2006, it is illegal to fund universities that the Secretary of State "knows or has reason to believe advocates, plans, sponsors, engages in, or has engaged in, terrorist activity."

After the publication of this book, Rice and her State Department comrades can no longer play stupid. If another cent of my hard-earned money goes to any of these universities, Congress had better pounce.

Things only take a downward spiral from here.

USAID in July 2005 held a ceremony marking contributions of $402,000 of our taxpayer dollars for the paving of the main street in Yaabid municipality, which is a major terrorist breeding ground just outside the West Bank city of Jenin.

Incredibly, in January 2007, the Palestinians renamed the U.S.-funded street after hanged Iraqi dictator Saddam Hussein!

Zacharias Zubeidi, leader of the Al Aqsa Martyrs Brigades in Yaabid and Jenin, told me the city changed the name on the U.S.-funded street to show "Saddam Hussein is still alive."

"We will honor his memory until the American and Zionist occupation is driven from our land," Zubeidi said.

USAID has multiple times paved streets and provided infrastructure in Gaza cities controlled by Hamas. Palestinians regularly throw USAID projects back in our faces.

After USAID funded road projects in Jenin in 2004, a central street there was named after the first Iraqi suicide bomber, who killed four American soldiers in Fallujah. The mayor of Jenin reportedly participated in an anti-American dedication ceremony in which speakers blessed the "resistance of the residents of Fallujah."

Also, a USAID-funded Palestinian sports center was named after Salef Khalef, operational head of the Black September terror organization, which was behind the killing of two U.S. diplomats in Sudan in 1973 and the massacre one year earlier of eleven Israeli Olympic athletes in Munich.

<>

I chose specifically to focus here on American funding of Palestinian terror because it is the arena I am closest to and know the most about. I don't feel comfortable accusing the U.S. of funding terrorism elsewhere, but I certainly am not surprised by the reports of America's backing of groups connected to terror all over the world, including in Iraq, Afghanistan, Kosovo, and other areas.

There have been reports the U.S. is funding violent Sunni groups connected to al-Qaida to stem the growth of Shiite influence in the Middle East. Some of the reports accuse America of pumping large sums of money, without congressional authority or oversight, for covert operations in the Middle East, including to groups wanting to take on Hezbollah and Iranian organizations.

Funding one terror group against another has never worked and always backfires. It results in more terror attacks, including attacks against Americans. It creates arms races with competing terror groups, which means still more killed in terrorist attacks. Why are we funding terror worldwide? Why are taxpayers letting the U.S. get away with this madness?

CHAPTER SEVEN

TERROR GRINCHES STEAL BETHLEHEM CHRISTMAS

A H, CHRISTMAS IN BETHLEHEM. Manger Square is ablaze with colorful lights. The weather is usually a bit chilly. Aggressive merchants bombard passersby with "special sales" on all kinds of cedar wood statues and religious carvings. And like clockwork, Middle East leaders and the mainstream media congregate every year to ignore rampant Muslim intimidation of Christians and instead blast Israel—often with completely inaccurate information—for ruining Christmas and for the drastic decline of Christianity in one of the holiest cities for that religion.

As a member of the media, I observed 2005 and 2006 midnight mass at Bethlehem's Church of the Nativity, which Christians believe is the birthplace of Jesus.

One after the other, speakers took the stage and resoundingly blamed Israel for fleeing Christians, mostly claiming a security barrier the Jewish state constructed in 2002 nearly ruined the city.

"Palestinians are seeking a bridge to peace instead of Israeli walls. Unfortunately, Israel is continuing with its destructive policy ... [and] transforming our land into a big jail," said U.S.-backed Palestinian President Mahmoud Abbas just prior to the mass services.

Delivering original sentiments, the Archbishop of Westminster, Cormac Murphy-O'Connor, urged Israel "to build bridges and not walls" and blamed Israel for "[compelling Christians] to leave the land of their birth for foreign lands on account of the political situation."

Jerusalem's Latin Patriarch Michel Sabbah, speaking at St. Catherine's Church, adjacent to the Church of the Nativity, called for Israel to remove its "separation barrier, which is causing all kinds of hardships and affecting normal life in Bethlehem."

Bethlehem is one of the oldest and most important Christian communities in the world. Christians composed upwards of 80 percent of Bethlehem when Israel was founded in 1948, but by 2006, they accounted for only 23 percent with a large majority of Muslims.

The 23 percent Christian statistic is generous since it includes the Bethlehem satellite towns of Beit Sahour and Beit Jala. Some estimates place Bethlehem's actual Christian population as low as 12 percent. If demographic trends continue, in about fifteen years there may be no Christians remaining in Bethlehem. Hundreds of Christians are fleeing Bethlehem every year.

The decline largely began in 1995, when Israel, which used to control Bethlehem, withdrew from the city, handing Bethlehem over to the Palestinian Authority as part of the U.S.-brokered 1993 Oslo Accords, which established a Palestinian fiefdom in the West Bank and Gaza Strip for PLO terror chief Yasser Arafat.

A few weeks after 2006 Christmas celebrations, I returned to Bethlehem and met with Ayman Abu Eita, who was chief of the Al Aqsa Martyrs Brigades terrorist group in Beit Sahour from 2001 until at least 2006. The Brigades, responsible for scores of suicide bombings, is the "military wing" of the Palestinian Fatah party. Beit Sahour neighbors Bethlehem to the east; for all intents and purposes the town is basically part of Bethlehem.

Eita was arrested by Israel several times for participation in terror activities, including scores of shooting attacks against Israelis, and was just released from prison a few days prior my meeting with him. He doesn't want to be arrested again any time soon so he asked that I don't label him as head of the Brigades in Beit Sahour, explaining to me he didn't participate in any attacks during the three days he had been out of jail. Instead Abu Eita wants me to introduce him as the main representative of PA President Mahmoud Abbas's Fatah party in Beit Sahour.

I drove down the narrow, ancient streets of Bethlehem and met Eita at a predetermined corner. He was driving a decent-looking Ford with two men inside. I couldn't tell if they were armed. I followed Eita by car to a building situated at a point which the tiny road we were traveling on came to a dead end.

Bethlehem's main shopping district is in shambles; the hotels, restaurants and apartments are mainly rundown, except of course for the homes of PA leaders, who tauntingly live in palaces fit for kings probably purchased with billions in the foreign aid Arafat and his Fatah gang hijacked from the Palestinian people. Bethlehem has so much potential. It could be one of the top tourist destinations for Christians worldwide. But it's not safe under Palestinian control.

I sat down in a comfortable living room with Eita, who, I must reiterate so he doesn't issue a *fatwa* against me, was not a terrorist on the day I met him. According to the Fatah representative, Israel is "one hundred percent" to blame for Christians running away from Bethlehem.

"Israel built a wall that strangles Bethlehem and brought down the economy. No one wants to visit. The Israelis come in and do military operations. The nature of Christians is they don't like instability. They don't like to live in an area where there are conflicts and problems. Israel is creating all the problems," said Eita.

Nice theory. But it'sit's a load of crock. Israel's security barrier in Bethlehem was built in 2002 to keep the city's terrorists from infiltrating Jewish towns. If indeed the security barrier was causing economic hardship prompting Christians to flee, the mass emigration of Bethlehem's Christians should have started after the barrier was constructed in 2002. But actually Bethlehem's Christian drastic decline curiously began seven years earlier, just after the Palestinians took control of the city.

Israel's barrier was constructed after the outbreak of Arafat's terror war in September 2000 after the PLO leader turned down an Israeli offer of a Palestinian state, returning to the Middle East to liberate Palestine with violence. Scores of deadly suicide bombings and shooting attacks against Israelis were planned in Bethlehem and carried out by Bethlehem-area terrorists, including Eita and his ilk.

At one point during the period of just thirty days in 2002, at least fourteen shootings were perpetuated by Fatah's Al Aqsa Martyrs Brigades in Bethlehem, killing two Israelis and wounding six. Many times Muslim gunmen in the Bethlehem area reportedly took positions in civilian homes in the hilltops of Christian Beit Jala, which straddles Bethlehem. Beit Jala afforded the terrorists a clear firing line at southern sections of Jerusalem and at a major Israeli highway down below, drawing Israeli military raids and the eventual building of the security barrier there.

I use the term "barrier," not "wall" because contrary to the claims of Palestinian leaders, repeated as fact by most major news media outlets, Israel did not build a wall that encircles Bethlehem. It built a fence only where the Bethlehem area interfaces with Jerusalem. A tiny segment of the barrier facing a major Israeli roadway is a concrete wall, which Israel says is meant to prevent gunmen from shooting at Israeli motorists.

But Eita maintained: "Israeli occupation is responsible for this bad situation [in Bethlehem]. Every day we see these soldiers here. When Arafat came at the beginning of Oslo, the security situation was very solid. We ruled and created stability."

I countered that Arafat brought nothing but horror to Bethlehem. As soon as he got his grimy terrorist hands on Bethlehem, Arafat unilaterally fired the city's Christian politicians and replaced them with Muslim cronies. He appointed a Muslim governor, Muhammed Rashad A-Jabar and deposed of Bethlehem's city council, which had nine Christians and two Muslims, reducing the number of Christians councilors to a 50-50 split.

Arafat then converted a Greek Orthodox monastery next to the Church of Nativity into his official Bethlehem residence.

Suddenly after the Palestinians gained the territory, reports of Christian intimidation by Muslims began to surface. Christian women were reportedly raped and stoned. Armed factions stirred tensions by holding militant demonstrations and marches in the streets. The armed Muslim intimidation demonstrations now happen regularly.

Arafat's PA was accused of stealing Christian land, a major problem still going on today.

"There are many cases where Christians have their land stolen by the Muslim mafia," said Samir Qumsiyeh, a Bethlehem

Christian leader and owner of the Beit Sahour-based private Al-Mahd (Nativity) TV station.

"It is a regular phenomenon in Bethlehem. They go to a poor Christian person with a forged power of attorney document, then they say we have papers proving you're living on our land. If you confront them, many times the Christian is beaten. You can't do anything about it. The Christian loses and he runs away," Qumsiyeh told me.

A 2007 *Jerusalem Post* article cited the case of Fuad and Georgette Lama, Christian residents of Bethlehem who said their land was stolen by the PA and when they tried to do something about it, Fuad was beaten by gunmen.

In America, if someone showed up at my home with a forged deed and threw me off my property, I'd go to the police and have the perpetrators immediately arrested. So why don't the Christians just complain to the authorities?

"What authorities?" asked Qumsiyeh, rhetorically. "You mean the security forces controlled by the Palestinian government, which is allowing this to happen? You mean the courts, which are controlled by the Palestinian government? It takes years to petition the court system and many times a verdict isn't even reached."

Qumsiyeh was one of the few Christian leaders in Bethlehem I met with who was willing to talk on the record about the *jihad* being waged against his religion in Jesus' believed birthplace. He has heroically delivered public speeches on the topic, but has paid the price. Locals recently attacked his home with Molotov cocktails.

"It was an absolute miracle I wasn't killed. Also my wife was outside at the time. My home has a big gas line that could have exploded. This is the price of speaking out in Bethlehem," he said.

Multiple Bethlehem Christians complained to me about land confiscations, saying several of their friends emigrated from Bethlehem after having their property stolen by Muslim thugs. I was told of instances in which Christians fled after they were falsely accused of selling property to Jews, a crime punishable by death in some Palestinian cities.

One religious novelty-store owner I met told me Muslim gangs regularly deface Christian property.

"We are harassed but you wouldn't know the truth. No one says anything publicly about the Muslims. This is why Christians are running away."

What? Muslim persecution is driving the Christians out of Bethlehem? One would never know that from the Christmas coverage by my colleagues in the media. Every year they spew the same "human interest stories" blaming only Israel. G-d forbid they should actually tell the world the true face of militant Islam. It doesn't take too much investigating in Bethlehem. Just walk around and ask the Christians.

During our meeting, Fatah's Eita told me Christians were making up stories about persecution.

"Most of those Christians who left Bethlehem gave the impression of persecution just as an excuse to justify why they left Bethlehem."

Thing is, Eita, I once personally witnessed the Muslim persecution of Bethlehem's Christians.

<><

In one of the scariest terror interviews I ever conducted, in April 2006, I met the senior leadership of Bethlehem's Al Aqsa Martyrs Brigades together with my friend, popular U.S. radio host Rusty Humphries. Humphries routinely travels to Israel for his show; together we do some pretty crazy things during the day and at night we host his show from a radio studio.

That particular day, we were supposed to meet Raad Abiat, leader of the Brigades in Bethlehem, to discuss with him the claims of Christian persecution at the hands of his terrorist group. But just minutes before we entered the city, Israel conducted an anti-terror raid in which Abiat was killed.

I received a phone call from the Brigades telling me of the killing. Since they like me, they offered a meeting instead with Abiat's second in command and cousin (they are all cousins), Abu Philistine, who immediately became Bethlehem's Brigades leader upon Abiat's death. I accepted.

After Abiat was killed, the mainstream media reported Bethlehem's Christians, in solidarity with the Brigades, closed down all schools, shops and institutions and declared a day of mourning and of anger toward Israel.

Actually, what really happened was the Brigades and other Palestinian law enforcers went up and down the streets and demanded all the Christian stores, restaurants, and schools close. Intimidating terrorists with guns ensured Christian institutions complied.

"We don't put up a fight. We just close the schools so there are no problems," a local Christian teacher told me.

But you'd never read that in the *NY Times*.

To further illustrate the biased, lying coverage of the media, *Reuters* and other news agencies reported Abiat, who they labeled a "militant," was gunned down by Israeli troops. They parroted claims by the PA that Abiat was unarmed and that he was chased from a local street to the roof of a Bethlehem building, where Israeli officers shot the unarmed Abiat to death and threw his bullet-ridden body off the roof to the ground below.

This was the same story Brigades leaders told me.

Well, Rusty and I showed up at the site where Abiat was killed. We watched family members enter a building and ascend to the roof to view the body.

I found an Abiat family member who spoke English.

"Why are you going to the roof to see the body? I thought he was thrown to the ground by the Israelis." I asked.

"No he wasn't. The body is still on the roof, where he was shot defending Palestinian honor," the family member told me proudly.

Outside the building were several witnesses to the violence. Rusty asked one of them if Abiat was armed when he was killed.

"Sure, he was carrying a machine gun and shooting at the Israelis. He also had something I am sure was an explosive device," said the witness.

The Israeli Defense Forces clarified they conducted a raid to arrest wanted terrorists, including Abiat, when Abiat opened fire and ran into the building. On the roof, Abiat was killed after firing several times at Israeli troops, who said he was carrying an explosive device.

Many English news media reports of Abiat's death cite the Palestinian claims unchallenged, and at the end of their absurd, lying articles, in a closing-note paragraph, stated the IDF version of events. Not one reporter bothered to simply check with Abiat's family or with witnesses. This is the state of most of our news media today.

Abiat was buried within two hours of his killing. Rusty wanted to attend the funeral, but the Brigades leaders said there would be a lot of anger expressed at Israel and America. They said if we attended they couldn't guarantee one of Abiat's relatives, many of whom are terrorists, wouldn't kill us in a moment of passion. Instead we watched from a main street as the funeral procession marched by. Dozens of cars brandishing Hamas and Fatah flags were followed by over a hundred gunmen, some shooting into the air.

After Abiat's funeral, Rusty and I set out to meet the new Bethlehem Brigades chief and his comrades. The terrorists told us to drive to a particular spot, pull over and stand near my Land Rover. We complied. A man who seemed in his mid-twenties passed us by, it turned out to scope the area for Israeli troops. The man was a new member of the Brigades; his face was likely unknown to the Israelis so he was sent to check for soldiers.

The young man returned and introduced himself to us as a member of the Brigades. He asked us to remove the batteries from our cell phones. Israel routinely uses cell phone signals to track wanted militants. The man, who was wielding a small black pistol, led Rusty and I about three hundred feet down a narrow Bethlehem ally, where he said his comrades would meet us.

While waiting, Rusty turned his back toward us and started taking pictures of the area. Then two terrorists armed with machine guns emerged and introduced themselves to me. One was the new Brigades leader, Abu Philistine. Rusty, though, was busy taking pictures. He didn't know the terrorists had arrived until he heard one of them cock his gun.

"As I'm taking a picture, I hear behind me click-click of a gun being cocked," Rusty relates. "It's a sound you never forget. And I'm thinking, oh no, we're dead. Then I turned around... They say you can't judge a book by its cover. Oh yeah you can. When I turned around I saw two of the meanest, scariest, dirtiest looking men I have ever seen."

They cocked their guns to be prepared. They were visibly jumpy, looking in all directions, scoping for Israelis. They told us they were extremely nervous about being assassinated after the Abiat killing.

All three terrorists were in their mid-twenties. Two were wearing jeans, one had on army fatigues. Their faces were grizzled and lightly bearded.

Abu Philistine told us the recorded interview could only last about ten minutes and that it had to take place outside.

My heart was pounding. I only fully realized upon arrival what a stupid idea it had been to meet nervous, armed terrorists whose leader had just been assassinated, but it was too late to go back.

Just before the start of our interview, we heard a door slam and all the terrorists quickly jolted, pointing their loaded weapons in the direction of the sound. I nearly had a heart attack. A young boy emerged, playing with a big red ball. The terrorists eased a bit. The boy saw the militants and the drawn guns but wasn't even mildly fazed. He stuck around. Life in Palestinian-controlled Bethlehem is full of terrorists and guns.

I began the interview formulaically, not even caring what I was asking. I just wanted to get out of Bethlehem.

"Are you persecuting Christians?" I asked, citing the rampant reports of intimidation and the history of Christianity's decline.

"Everything you say is Israeli propaganda. There is no Christian persecution anywhere. Christians and Muslims are all part of the Palestinian people and we have the same goals to live in freedom and solidarity," replied Abu Philestine.

When he finished responding, we heard a rustling noise. Abu Philestine pointed his gun in the direction of the sound. A stray cat emerged. Israel is filled with stray felines. Rusty and I were both freaked out.

"You know, I saw gunmen today march through the streets. I was told they were ensuring all the establishments were closed for the funeral," I said, biting back my words.

"We have our rules in Bethlehem and one of them is shops must be closed if one of our heroes is killed by the Zionists. We don't enforce anything. All the people here are on our side," Abu Philestine claimed.

Sure, they're all with you, I thought. Then why do you need intimidating men with guns enforcing a closure? I didn't ask because I was scared. I just allowed him to continue speaking.

Abu Philestine gave me the usual party lines for the remainder of our very brief, nerve-wracking interview—the Jews drove out the Christians; everything is honky dory in Christian town; Muslim intimidation is all a bunch of Israeli propaganda.

Rusty and I raced out of that interview while the Brigades leaders went about their business of intimidating Christians, stealing property, and shooting at Israelis from Christian neighborhoods.

Though I departed Bethlehem, my heart remained there. On the drive back, I told Rusty I couldn't help but feel partially responsible for the plight of the Christians we had just visited. After all it was my American government that backed the Oslo Accords and brokered the deal that compelled Israel to withdraw from Bethlehem and turn the sacred city over to some of the most anti-Christian thugs ever to grace planet earth.

Though they would not say it on the record, every Christian in Bethlehem I spoke to affirmed they want Israel to retake Bethlehem.

Qumsiyeh told me he appealed to U.S. Christian leaders to help initiate housing projects and find ways to fortify and strengthen Bethlehem's Christian population.

"The way things are, soon there will not be a single Christian living in the land of Jesus," he said.

Muslims Shout at Jesus' Home: "Islam Will Dominate the World!"

Young Muslim men, some in battle gear marched down Nazareth's main thoroughfare beating drums as a man on loudspeaker repeatedly exclaimed in Arabic, "Allah is great." Leaders of the Islamic Movement, a major Muslim political party, paraded down the street brandishing their party's green flag. Hundreds of activists strutted screaming Islamist epithets, including "Islam is the only truth" and "Islam shall rule all."

Tens of thousands, seemingly mostly Muslim residents of Nazareth, congregated on the streets as the march passed, cheering on the parade.

The Islamic Movement said it organized the march, which took place the night before 2007's New Years Eve, to celebrate Eid ul-Adha, or the Feast of the Sacrifice, which commemorates the Muslim belief Abraham was willing to sacrifice his son Ishmael for Allah. (Of course, I reject this—it was Isaac, not Ishmael, whom Abraham almost sacrificed.)

While the march was billed as a celebration, its militant virtues were clearly visible. The event seemed more a show of Islamic force than a street party.

It took place in one of the holiest cities for Christians. Nazareth, which just one hundred years ago was almost entirely Christian, is described in the New Testament as the childhood home of Jesus. It contains multiple important shrines and churches, including the famous Church of the Basilica of the Annunciation, the site at which many Christians believe the Virgin Mary was visited by the Archangel Gabriel and told that she had been selected as the mother of Jesus.

Most of Nazareth's dwindling, nearly extinct Christian population stayed away from the Muslim march, with the exception of a few Christian shopkeepers who worked on the main street, where the militant parade was taking place.

I marched alongside the front of the parade, with quite a few marchers assuming I was Muslim. After one of the participants heard me speak English with my thick American accent, he inquired where I was from and asked which mosque I attend in the U.S. I pretended I couldn't hear him above the sound of the gathering. He continued beating his drums.

I bore witness as the march reached its crescendo at the main shopping area, just outside a series of Christian stores. The Christian shopkeepers observed from inside their boutiques as the militant Muslim parade proclaimed the exclusivity of Allah and Muhammad on loudspeakers. I will never forget the look of absolute horror on most of the shopkeepers' faces. Their glares for me are frozen in event and memory, calcified and motionless in a story of centuries-old intimidation and persecution that was highlighted on that night. The Christians didn't have to say anything. Their expressions said it all. They know the tide in Nazareth is quickly rising against them.

I observed and quickly snapped a picture as several Muslim youth marching in the parade started to charge at three local Christian shopkeepers who courageously stood outside their shops. But the youth stopped short.

The Muslim children were a rowdy bunch. They were running back and forth. Some were launching firecrackers into the sky, occasionally misfiring, sending the small explosives shooting dangerously close to the crowds. Kids who could not have been above the age of ten were activating firecrackers. I was frightened one would take my eye out. Actually, I was more afraid of the kids misfiring the explosives than I was of most of the terrorists I ever met.

Earlier in the day I met with Saleem, a Nazareth Christian resident who asked that his last name be withheld for fear of what he said was "Muslim retaliation" for speaking out. We had coffee in a Christian-owned shop, where he felt more at liberty to talk.

"Tonight's march is meant to intimidate Christians. It's part of the methods used by the Muslims in very obvious ways to create an atmosphere where the Christians should know the Muslims are the main power and we are not welcome anymore," said Saleem.

Saleem and several other Christians in Nazareth spoke of attacks against Christian-owned shops and told stories of Christian women being raped by Muslim men. They noted several instances of interreligious violence and Muslim riots they said began when Muslims attacked Christian worshippers. The Muslims claimed Christians started the violence.

Israeli security officials say the majority of anti-Christian violence in Nazareth goes unreported because local Christians are too afraid to report crimes.

One Christian resident said violence and intimidation tend to increase around the time of local elections. The Islamic parties, once in the minority, are now one seat away from dominating Nazareth's city council.

"During the last elections, Muslims on the streets were threatening the Christians. They tried to stop some of the Christian cars from voting," said Saleem.

In October 2000, the Arab Christian mayor of Nazareth, Ramiz Jaraisy, was reportedly beaten by members of the opposing Islamist party.

Ahmed Zohbi, a member of Nazareth's municipal council and the leader of an umbrella group consisting of the city's Islamic parties, denied Saleem's accusations, claiming there is "no problem" between Christians and Muslims in Nazareth.

"We just want to celebrate," Zohbi told me. "The Muslims have nothing against our Christian brothers. Our communities may have differences but we live a peaceful coexistence."

Zohbi said Muslims have no intention of taking over Nazareth. He attributed the city's dying Christian population to "economics."

"Christians want to be where the good life is. They're moving to other cities," he said.

I agreed with Zohbi that Christians likely do want to be where the good life is. But to them a good life means freedom from intimidation.

Nazareth, an ancient town, is entirely controlled by Israel, but the Jewish state largely stays away from the city's affairs and internal Christian-Muslim disputes. The beautiful city is nestled in a hollow plateau some twelve hundred feet above sea level, located between large, forested high hills that form the most southerly points of the Lebanon mountain range. It's about ten miles from the Sea of Galilee and about four miles west of Mount Tabor.

Israel's Central Bureau of Statistics reported in 2004 Nazareth's Christian population was about twenty thousand people out of a total population of around seventy thousand, making Christians slightly less than 30 percent of Nazareth's total population.

That number represents a complete reversal in demography. The *Jewish Encyclopedia* of 1906 states there were ten thousand people in Nazareth; thirty-five hundred Muslim "and the rest Christians."

What caused all the Christians to vacate Nazareth?

"They want bigger houses. They want more culture. Nazareth isn't so luxurious anymore," Zohbi told me with a straight face just prior to the parade, as militant Muslims hung a big sign a few feet from where we were speaking that read, "Islam is the only truth."

The situation for Christians took a turn for the worst in perhaps one of the most threatening anti-Christian moves in Nazareth and one that should concern every Christian worldwide. In December 1997, a gang of Muslims gathered at the foot of the Church of the Annunciation, one of the holiest Christian sites, and unilaterally declared the area part of the *waqf*, or Muslim trust.

As they always do with major sacred sites of other religions, the Muslims claimed the site outside the church is really a Muslim holy area. They found some guy who is supposedly buried there and who they say is Shabeldin, a warrior and the nephew of Saladin, the Muslim commander who led the army that defeated the Crusaders in 1187. The site previously housed a public school.

The Muslims erected a tent outside the church as a temporary mosque and announced plans to build a huge mosque with an eighty-six-foot minaret in honor of Shabeldin. Islamic Movement leaders demanded Nazareth officials deed the property over to local Muslim authorities.

Dave Parsons, a spokesman for the International Christian Embassy, said the proposed mosque might contain multiple spires that would tower over the Annunciation Church's large, black-coned dome.

There are plenty of dead Muslims who are nephews of other dead Muslims at whose gravesites a mosque can be built, but no, the Muslims of Nazareth only want to build this imposing mosque right in front of the Church of the Annunciation.

Two years later, in April 1999, the Muslims rioted outside the church because they know violence works when it comes to intimidating the Israeli government. According to reports, Muslim gangs targeted property displaying Christian symbols and Christian holy sites.

BBC News reported:

> Some [Muslims] hurled insults and curses at worshippers as they left the church, where Roman Catholics believe the angel Gabriel appeared before Mary and told her she was pregnant. Other youths, wielding clubs, smashed windshields of cars with crosses dangling from the mirrors. Police said thirty cars were damaged.

> Protesters spray-painted his name [Shabeldin, the Muslim believed to be buried near the Church] across an ancient well where Orthodox Christians believe Mary drew her water and the annunciation took place.

Of course the Muslims claimed Christian teenagers started the riots.

Two weeks after the riots, the Israeli government caved into the Muslim demands and approved the plan to construct the intimidation mosque in front of the church.

But in 2002, then–Prime Minister Ariel Sharon rescinded permission to construct the mosque following worldwide outcry and protests from the Vatican and White House.

In our interview, Zohbi credited "American conservatives," particularly "big U.S. radio hosts," with helping stop the construction of the mosque.

But the Muslims continue to demand the mosque be built. Since the Christian population is dwindling, it is very likely an umbrella Muslim political party will take control of the city's municipality in near future elections, deed the site outside the church over to Muslim groups, and grant permission for the mosque's construction, which would require the Israeli government to intercede, and who knows whether that will happen again.

Zohbi told me he is "optimistic" the mosque will eventually be built.

"It's just a matter of time before we [the Islamic parties] dominate the city council and then the situation will be different," he said.

The day I met him, hundreds of Muslims held prayer services outside the church at the site they demand for the new mosque. They hold the services every day. In a clear statement, Muslim men congregate outside the holy Christian site to pray facing away from the church. Their backsides are flashed to the church as they bow to Allah.

On the day I attended services, a sermon was delivered by a prominent local *sheik*, who shouted into a microphone attached to several large speakers, "Islam will dominate the world." My translator Ali, who was present, told me the speech was Islamist and demanded the world recognize the "giant, Islam."

The speech could be heard from inside the Annunciation church. I watched a few nuns pass the sermon very quickly, looking the other way, seemingly deliberately trying not to attract attention to themselves. I am told these kinds of sermons are delivered on loudspeakers in front of the church every Friday.

◇

The conflict against the church and against Nazareth's Christians didn't start in the 1990s or even this century. Islam's trying to destroy the Annunciation Church dates back thousands of years.

As early as 725 CE, Willibald, the eighth-century bishop of Eichstätt, noted on his visit to Nazareth that only the Church of the Annunciation stood at the center of the city. He said of the church, "Christians often redeemed from the Saracens [a term for the Arab Empire under the Umayyad and Abbasid *caliphates*], when they threatened to destroy it."

Archeologists say the first shrine at the church site was constructed in the middle of the fourth century, comprising an altar in the cave in which Mary is said to had lived. Several previous churches there date back to the fifth century, about the same time the Church of the Nativity was constructed in Bethlehem.

The original Annunciation church was destroyed by Caliph Hakim who began a decade-long persecution of Christians.

1263 CE saw the destruction of all church and non-Muslim sacred structures of Nazareth at the hands of Sultan Baybars, a thirteenth-century Mamluk sultan of Egypt and Syria.

Reconstructed versions of the Annunciation church were burned during Crusader losses in the region. The church was rebuilt again in 1730, then later enlarged in 1877.

The church structure was completely rebuilt in 1955. And this rebuilding is used by modern Nazareth Muslim leaders to claim the church has no historic ties to Jesus.

Zohbi claimed the Muslim stake to the Nazareth church site predates Christianity's. He said the Church of the Annunciation "was built in the 1950s."

Siham el-Fahum, a Muslim Nazareth municipality member and a local historian, actually admits Christians are fleeing her city because Christian-Muslim tension.

I met her at a local Nazareth eatery.

"There is no doubt the situation for Christians in Nazareth is bad," El-Fahum said. "Muslims in the city want more dominance and the only way to achieve that, logically, is at the expense of Christians. It's a delicate balancing act that is having negative consequences for Christians."

Like many Muslims here, El-Fahum claimed Christians several times "instigated" Muslim riots. But she said in the struggle for power, "Muslims are definitely on the rise."

Zohbi earlier said he would only lead "peaceful" protests to build the mosque. Muslims in Nazareth have "no interest" in tensions or further violence with local Christians, he claimed.

But El-Fahum said it was only a matter of time before another round of anti-Christian riots was sparked.

"The tension is very palatable. The Christians know it. The situation is a powder keg that can explode again at any time."

◇

The trend of the persecution and intimidation of Christians in Bethlehem and Nazareth is part of a larger story of *jihad* against non-Muslims being waged by Islam throughout the Middle East and around the world.

Ever since Israel withdrew from the Gaza Strip in August 2005, Islamic groups there have been targeting Christian institutions, firebombing churches and Christian bookstores, even shooting up a United Nations school, absurdly accusing the evil world body of spreading Christianity! Israel had to ethnically cleanse Gaza of its Jews before handing the territory to the Palestinians, knowing full well any Jew that remained would have undoubtedly been savaged.

After Syria was forced to withdraw its troops from Lebanon in 2005, the Lebanese were rocked by a series of bombings widely blamed on Damascus and viewed as an attempt to destabilize Lebanon. But what no one pointed out is the vast majority of bombings—and there have been many—have targeted Christian neighborhoods.

Christians previously made up the majority of Lebanon's population. A 1932 census stated Lebanon was 55 percent Christian. But recent surveys cited by the CIA Factbook state Muslims now constitute a solid majority with 60 percent..

After a bombing ripped through his Christian town, Samy Gemayel, brother of assassinated Lebanese politician Pierre Gemayel and son of Lebanon's former president Amin Gemayel, told me Christians are being driven from Lebanon.

"These bombings are intimidating Christians and also Lebanese in general," said Gemayel. "Ninety percent of all the assassinations the past two years and most of the bombings have occurred in Christian population centers."

"You don't hear this on the news too often, but I'm telling you, Christians are fleeing Lebanon. It's a major problem," Gemayel said.

In Syria, all religious groups must register with the government and obtain government permits to hold any meeting other than pre-approved worship services. The Syrian government reportedly has attempted to control places of worship, monitoring sermons and services.

There have been reports of Christians being intimidated, abducted, and held for ransom by Muslims in Iraq, even under U.S. occupation. Churches have been bombed, Christian businesses shut down. In 2005 alone, thirty thousand Christians fled Iraq, according to survey information. The U.S.-backed Iraqi government's constitution establishes Islam as the official state religion and allows for the appointment to Iraq's highest court judges whose only expertise are in Islamic *sharia* law.

In Iran, where Islamic law is imposed, the government is accused of regularly harassing Christian institutions; its "Ministry of Islamic Guidance" is charged with monitoring all non-Muslim religions' organizations. The printing of Christian literature, including church newsletters, is strictly forbidden. Muslims who convert to Christianity are subject to the death penalty.

The Christian Copts of Egypt are regularly singled out and targeted. Restrictions are imposed on rebuilding or repairing churches. Egypt has effectively banned Christians from senior government, military or educational positions; its state-run media spews vicious anti-Christian and anti-Semitic propaganda.

And we tend to forget about one of the most massive recent targeting of non-Muslims in the Middle East—the Arab world's expulsion of nearly 99 percent of its Jews after Israel was founded in 1948. So much is said about Israel supposedly displacing Palestinians; what about the Arab displacement of Jews?

The theme goes on and on. Still, our senior politicians regularly meet and take photo ops with Arab leaders but rarely bring up their regime's ill treatment of non-Muslims. Still, the U.S. considers Egypt an ally and provides it with billions in aid. Still, many are calling for engagement with Iran and Syria, emboldening those countries to believe they are above the norms of civilized society. Still, the American government pressures Israel to withdraw from more lands knowing full well the fate of all the non-Muslims who are left behind.

CHAPTER EIGHT

"ANOTHER 9/11 ON ITS WAY"

WAR LESSONS FROM TERRORISTS

"THEY PUT ME IN A SMALL BOX and poured in masses of roaches and all kind of insects to freak me out, but that didn't much bother me," said G. Gordon Liddy, the popular U.S. radio talk host, actor and notorious mastermind of the first break-in of the Democratic National Committee headquarters in the Watergate building in 1972.

"I don't have any problem with insects because I used to sleep with them in prison. Once while incarcerated I woke up at night feeling there was a blanket on me. I determined the blanket was made of live cockroaches. I brushed them off and went to bed," related Liddy, who was the former chief operative for President Richard Nixon's White House Plumbers unit. He served four and a half years of a twenty-year sentence for his role in Watergate, later being commuted by President Jimmy Carter.

"Next they heated the little box and I was fine with that," Liddy said in his trademark calm, quiet demeanor. "Afterwards they threw in some electric shocks and piped in all sorts of fowl smelling odors, but it didn't faze me. You've never smelled a terrible odor until you've spent time in our federal prison system."

Liddy, myself, Liddy's feisty, trigger-happy Canadian producer, Franklin Raff, and my translator Ali were cruising in my Land Rover on a slightly chilly Friday morning in December up the coast of Israel toward the border with Syria and Lebanon. It had been five months since Israel essentially failed to win the 2006 war in Lebanon against the Lebanese Hezbollah militia; Liddy and I were slated to meet with a leader of a new purported copycat Syrian guerilla organization modeling itself after Hezbollah and threatening eminent "resistance" against the Jewish state.

Liddy is kind enough to feature me on his radio show regularly. When he visits Israel, we spend time together and he accompanies me on some of my adventures.

On the long drive to the northern tip of Israel, Liddy regaled us with his experience competing a few months earlier in NBC's *Celebrity Fear Factor*. Liddy, who was seventy-five during the show's taping, beat out contestants one-third his age, winning all challenges except the final competition, which required good night vision.

"You must have the mindset that you will win," said Liddy. "Not that you'll survive but that you will prevail. If you think you will win, you probably will. This is the problem with the Israeli government. They lost their victory mentality of the past and now it's all about staying in power and surviving the next crisis."

Soon after Liddy's appropriate anecdote was offered, we arrived at our destination, the Golan Heights home of a representative of Syrian President Bashar Assad's Baath party and a leader of a new purported guerilla group.

The Heights is strategic mountainous territory looking down on Israeli and Syrian population centers twice used by Damascus to launch ground invasions into the Jewish state. Israel captured the Golan Heights in 1967, after Syria attacked, and again in 1973 following a war in which Syria used the territory to attack a second time. Since then, Syria, which is in an official state of war with Israel and supports the Jewish state's enemies, has been demanding Israel relinquish the strategic land. Israel officially annexed the Golan in 1981 and controls the territory. The United Nations considers the area disputed territory that should be given to Syria under a peace treaty.

Approximately eighteen thousand Jews live in beautiful, developed communities in the Golan, which has an Arab population of about seventeen thousand. The Arab residents retain their Syrian citizenship but under Israeli law can also sue for Israeli citizenship.

The Baath representative who doubles as a leader of the new purported Syrian guerilla group greeted us as we parked our car. He agreed to the meeting under the condition his full name be withheld, even though he is one of the only Baath officials living in the Golan and all are well known to the Israeli security apparatus.

"Welcome to Syria," said the official, laughing, shaking our hands.

"Soon, very soon, this entire territory will be returned to its rightful owners," he said.

A lot of people wrongly think the Golan Heights was in Syrian hands forever. Actually, the plateau, rising three thousand feet above the plains of Galilee, was governed by Israel longer than Damascus, and at least part was stolen from the Jews.

Syria only held the Golan for nineteen years until Israel first captured it. Tens of thousands of acres of Golan farmland was legally purchased by Jews as far back as the late nineteenth century. The Turks of the Ottoman Empire kicked out some of them around the turn of the century. But much of this land was still farmed until 1947 when Syria first became an independent state and quickly seized the land that was being worked by the Jewish Palestine Colonization Association and the Jewish Colonization Association.

Still, the international community considers the Golan to be Syrian.

The Baath official directed us to a modest sized workroom above his house. The place was scantily furnished in Druze decor, a computer was buzzing in the background. The walls were plastered with Syrian propaganda posters and pictures of Bashar Assad and Bashar's late father, Hafez.

"If in the coming months an agreement is not forged between Israel and Syria [for an Israeli withdrawal from the Golan], we will begin attacks," said the official, as he poured each of us tea.

The official told us Syria watched as Israel "lost" a war against the Lebanese Hezbollah militia in the summer of 2006 and noted that Syria learned that "fighting" is more effective than peace negotiations with regard to gaining territory.

Hezbollah, which seeks the destruction of Israel, claims its goal is to liberate the Shebaa Farms, a small, twelve-square-mile bloc situated between Syria, Lebanon, and Israel. A cease-fire resolution accepted by Israel to end its military campaign in Lebanon calls for negotiations leading to Israel's relinquishing of the Shebaa Farms.

"A cease fire was imposed after heavy fighting. If Syria does the same thing, if we wage a war against Israel, we'll get the Golan back in the cease fire," said the Baath official.

To that effect, he explained to us elements in Syria formed a new guerilla group, the Committees for the Liberation of the Golan Heights, which he said will initiate Hezbollah-like attacks against Israel in hopes of eventually provoking a conflict or generating leftist domestic Israeli pressure for Israel to vacate the Golan.

Syria is completely state-controlled. It quickly squashes any major opposition. No terror group can possibly be formed there without the sanctioning of the government. Indeed, I was told if I wanted to interview the overall leader of the new Committees, who resides in Damascus, I'd have to first be approved by the Syrian government.

After we finished our tea, the official hopped in my now crowded car and escorted us on a tour of the Golan. Only this wasn't your ordinary sightseeing tour. We were brought to particular areas the official told us were possible points at which the Committees may initiate attacks.

He directed us to the very top of the Golan, to a strategic outlook center at which one can see deep inside Syria, Lebanon, and Israel.

"You see that Jewish community down there?" the official asked, pointing in the direction of a visible Jewish town. "It's one of several that we can infiltrate and attack."

The official said there are multiple points of vulnerability along the Syria-Israel border that can be exploited. A lot of the Golan is situated much higher than Syria, but some sections are at level.

According to the official, the Committees is training for attacks in Syria.

"We know from history guerilla resistance works against Israel," said the official.

Syria accepted a United Nations ceasefire in October 1973, it waged a sporadic guerilla campaign against Israeli troops in the Golan until a disengagement agreement was reached March 31, 1974, that saw Israel withdraw from some sections of the territory.

"War is coming," said the Baath official. "It's inevitable."

The Baath official said Damascus is preparing for a larger war with the Jewish state in the "very near future."

"More and more of our units have undergone intensive trainings starting at 6 a.m. and finishing late into the evening. If the need arises, we are ready for a war," said the official.

The official said Syria "learned from the Hezbollah experience last summer and we can have hundreds of missiles hitting Tel Aviv that will overwhelm Israel's anti-missile batteries."

Whether the Committees for the Liberation of the Golan Heights launches attacks, whether Syria provokes Israel into war, these players are part of a larger picture that greatly affects the U.S. and could potentially drastically change the landscape of the Middle East and the larger geopolitical map.

If one takes a step back, if one observes the momentum in the Middle East, particularly coming from Iran's proxies in Iraq, Syria, Lebanon, the West Bank and Gaza, and from Iran itself, the picture that is painted is one of a region inching closer to a possible major confrontation with the West.

According to security officials, politicians and even militant leaders I spoke to—including senior terrorists backed by Iran—war may be around the corner.

And if we want to win, if we want to be victorious in Iraq and in the greater war on terror, there are certain lessons the terrorists taught to me that we must quickly incorporate into our battle plan. Here are a few important ones:

Lesson #1: Cease fires: 'chance to reload'

In a briefing with reporters in May, 2007, Lt. Gen. Raymond Odierno, one of the top American commanders in Iraq, announced that U.S. commanders at all levels are being empowered to reach out for truce talks with Iraqi insurgents, militants, tribes, thieves, religious leaders and sectarian rivals in a bid to end attacks against our troops.

"We are talking about cease-fires and maybe signing some things that say they won't conduct operations against the government of Iraq or against coalition forces," Odierno told reporters in a video conference from Baghdad.

"[Iraqi] Prime Minister Maliki and the government of Iraq have to continue to reach out to all these groups…bringing these groups into the political process so we can deal with their differences in a peaceful way instead of in violent ways," Odierno said.

The belief terrorists are interested in cease fires is commonly held by the West. Top senators and congressmen regularly urge truce talks with Iraqi insurgents, terror groups and the world's top state sponsors of terrorism. Some members of the European Union believe Hamas, which seeks the destruction of Israel, is interested in serious negotiations and in moderation. France recently invited the Lebanese Hezbollah terror group to join in the political discourse with regard to the future of Lebanon.

I asked the terrorists what they thought of the concept of a truce in which one side agrees to cease hostilities and anti-terror operations in exchange for an end to terrorism.

The militant leaders were overjoyed when they heard Odierno's announcement of American willingness to reach a cease fire in Iraq: Muhammad Abdel-Al, spokesman and a leader of the Popular Resistance Committees terror group, called truce talks with insurgents "a big victory for the resistance."

"Americans are recognizing the resistance, the same resistance that they before called terrorism; now they are dealing with these groups, and this (Odierno announcement) is the recognition of the Iraqi resistance and recognition by the Americans of their own losses in Iraq," said Abdel-Al.

"This [talk of a cease fire] is a great achievement for the resistance in Iraq and this achievement will be complimented by more and more dead American soldiers they will carry in coffins to the U.S.," Abdel-Al said.

Nasser Abu Aziz, the deputy commander of the Al Aqsa Martyrs Brigades in the northern West Bank, said talks with Iraqi militants "shows America is recognizing its failure in Iraq and that the invasion of Iraq was judged by Allah to be a failure. This is a great victory for the resistance."

Abu Abdullah, a leader of Hamas's so-called military wing in the Gaza Strip, said the negotiation of a cease-fire in Iraq "is proof that Iraq will be the end of America."

"The Americans didn't achieve anything with this invasion but to bring about their downfall."

Abu Abdullah said violence in Iraq will continue regardless of a cease-fire.

"Of course the resistance will continue," he said.

Still, according to the terrorists, a cease fire has great value. They explained to me Islam doesn't believe in cease fires. The Arabic word for truce is *hudna*, which in the Quran is a temporary respite to prepare for the continuation of attacks so the enemy can be destroyed.

The terrorists told me a truce with a non-Muslim enemy can extend up to ten years, but usually no more, and that in the end the enemy must be defeated.

In the Quran, the terrorists explained, Muhammad in the seventh century agreed to a famous cease fire—the Truce of Hudaybiyah—with the attacking Quraysh tribe of Mecca for ten years.

Hudaybiyah is a small oasis between Mecca and Medina where Muhammad fought a battle in the early years of Islam. When he saw he was losing, Muhammad signed a strategic ten-year peace agreement with the Quraish tribe living in Mecca. Two years later, when his forces were stronger and the Meccans were living securely and off their guard, Muhammad marched into the city and captured it.

The terrorists explained in Islam there is a principle known as Takiya, the right to "fake" peace when you are weak for the purposes of defeating your enemy when you are stronger.

This religious doctrine is applied all the time by our enemies.

In November 2006, for example, Israel agreed to a cease-fire with terrorists in the Gaza Strip. Prime Minister Ehud Olmert announced the cessation of all Israeli military operation in Gaza in exchange for vows of quiet from terror groups. The terror leaders were overjoyed. They needed a brief respite from Israeli ops. They told me they would use the time off to smuggle weapons; reinforce and train "fighters;" and produce rockets, mortars and all kinds of munitions for a future confrontation.

"The cease-fire offers a period of calm for our fighters to re-cover and prepare for our final goal of evacuating Palestine," said the Committees's Abdel-Al.

"We will keep fighting [Israel], but for the moment we will postpone certain parts of the military struggle. We will reinforce very quickly and rush what we are doing to prepare [for attacks]."

Hamas' Abu Abdullah said his terror group agreed to the cease-fire "because we need a period of calm to recuperate. This lull in fighting will not bring us to speak about peace."

Abu Luay, a leader of Islamic Jihad in Gaza, told me his ter-ror group's attacks against Israel would resume "at a time of our choosing."

Indeed, it has resumed with a vengeance.

Lesson #2: Unilateral withdrawal means victory for terror. Evacu-ated territory will be used to attack you.

"The jihadists [are] in Iraq. But that doesn't mean we stay there. They'll stay there as long as we're there," said then-House Minor-ity Leader Nancy Pelosi in a 2006 60 Minutes interview.

Sen. John F. Kerry and many of his colleagues in 2007 called for the withdrawal of twenty thousand troops from Iraq before year's end and a timetable for a complete retreat from the terri-tory, stating an evacuation would enhance U.S. security. And why not? Al-Qaida constantly states one of its main gripes is the U.S. occupation of Iraq, even though the terror group repeatedly attacked us long before Baghdad was a glimmer in George W. Bush's eye; even though the invasion of Iraq was in stated re-sponse to the global jihad group's mega-terror attacks on Sep-tember 11.

Reacting to the withdrawal talk, Muhammad Saadi, a senior leader of Islamic Jihad in the northern West Bank town of Jenin, said calls for an American evacuation from Iraq makes him feel "proud."

"As Arabs and Muslims we feel proud of this talk. Very proud from the great successes of the Iraqi resistance. This success that brought the big superpower of the world to discuss a possible withdrawal."

I asked Saadi whether a unilateral withdrawal from Iraq would end worldwide terrorism. Laughing, he responded, "There is no chance that the resistance will stop."

He said an American withdrawal from Iraq would "prove the resistance is the most important tool and that this tool works. The victory of the Iraqi revolution will mark an important step in the history of the region and in the attitude regarding the United States."

Former Al Aqsa Martyrs Brigades chieftain in Bethlehem Jihad Jaara said an American withdrawal from Iraq would "mark the beginning of the collapse of this tyrant empire [America]."

For anyone believing unilateral pullouts work, take a long look at the Gaza Strip. Prior to Israel's historic evacuation of Gaza in August 2005, terror leaders there announced their groups would build armies in Gaza and use the territory to attack Israel and further their goal of destroying the Jewish state.

Still, Israel retreated. Boasting of victory, Hamas was immediately elected to power and now launches regular rocket attacks against nearby Jewish population centers. Palestinian groups reportedly smuggled hundreds of tons of weaponry into Gaza, formed advanced armies, built military fortifications, and now are poised to launch a major confrontation with Israel.

Most of the terrorists I talked to were convinced the U.S. would shortly pull out of Iraq.

Ramadan Adassi, leader of the Al Aqsa Martyrs Brigades in the Asqar refugee camp in the West Bank, commented, "The Americans are losing and they will keep losing and very soon will be compelled to retreat. We can see that America failed at imposing its hegemony in Iraq."

Abu Mosaab, a commander of Islamic Jihad's Al Quds Brigades in the West Bank, said, "At the end of the day, the U.S. will leave and the Islamic resistance will win. It is very obvious that this is happening now and will be accelerated in the coming months."

Lesson #3: Rename the "war on terror"

Okay, so the terrorists say cease-fires don't work and withdrawals will be used to further war. How then can we defeat terrorism? I actually asked the terrorists to explain how we can destroy them. They pointed out something I believe we must take into account.

Speaking to a panel of terror leaders assembled for this book, I petitioned each individually: "I know that this is crazy to ask you, but let's say our goal is the destruction of al-Qaida and all groups like it. How should America beat al-Qaida? How should we beat them militarily? Give us advice. How can we win our war on terror?"

Hamas's Abu Abdullah responded, "About your so-called war on terrorism, how can you fight an idea? Of course your government is the biggest terrorist gang in the world, Israel is the second, and Great Britain is the third. But if you insist on calling us terrorists and waging a war against us, then say so. Don't be cowards and say you are fighting an idea."

Islamic Jihad's Abu Mosaab agreed: "What you Americans are stupid about and don't understand is that you can't fight a military war on your stupid term terrorism. It's impossible."

Continued Mosaab: "Anyway, you are fighting Al Qaida, which represents Allah's will. You fight for your own materialistic reasons. But Al-Qaida and insurgents and the Palestinian resistance is fighting for Allah and is looking to die, to be killed as a *shaheed*. How can you use your military might to defeat somebody that goes out from a hole, launches a mortar against a tank, and disappears among millions? Don't you see, we won't stop fighting until victory."

Al Aqsa's Adassi said much the same thing.

"After we put aside that you are the terrorists and we are resistance movements leading a legitimate religious war that will not accept any compromise, I must say how foolish it is of Bush to launch a war against something called terror," said Adassi.

Lesson #4: Islamic terror groups share the same goal

Terrorism in Israel is different from terrorism in London or New York. Terrorists in Iraq have a completely different agenda from those bombing Lebanon or Egypt or Jordan. *Sunni* terror and *Shiah* terror are totally different.

I cannot tell you the number of times I've heard these arguments from American columnists, television news panelists, politicians, so-called terror experts, or even some of my friends. There is a predominant belief that terrorism is regional and that various terror groups don't share the same goals.

The terrorists scoffed at this argument.

"It's really ridiculous," Islamic Jihad's Abu Mosaab told me. "Yes, we all need to fight the *jihad* locally. Yes, there is Shia Hezbollah and Sunni Hamas. My goal for now is to liberate Palestine. In Iraq, the *mujaheedeen* [fighters] must rid the region of American occupation. There is the fight against traitor governments, like Egypt and Saudi Arabia, but it's the same fight. The defeat of the anti-Muslim world."

"We are in World War Three," he said. "The Americans are doing everything to prevent Islam to emerge as the world superpower and you are carrying out a policy of injustice against Muslims. But there is one basic fact and that is all groups have the same goal and we know that Allah will bring victory to the believers, and I am telling you that you are fighting Allah, not Islam. And Allah is invincible."

Al Aqsa Brigades leader Adassi said "there is one fight for all Islamic resistance and that is the fight for Islamic rule and all the signs prove that we are going towards a comprehensive confrontation."

Adassi warned, "For the moment, the Americans are enjoying the fact that only a minority of fighters are fighting them, but this is changing, and once the change is deep and the Muslims will wake up from their indifference, the victory will no doubt be to Islam and the defeat to the U.S. and its allies. This is a world war."

Meir Amit, legendary former director of Israel's Mossad intelligence agency, is one of the few major analysts to acknowledge the state of affairs of which the terrorists say they are extremely aware.

"We are on the eve of war with the Islamic world, which will wage a war and all kinds of actions and attacks against the Western world. We already noticed the terrorists in the world hit Spain, England, France. I call it World War III. You must look at it from this angle and treat it wider, not as a problem of terrorism here and there," Amit told me during a radio interview.

The former intelligence chief, who directed some of the most notorious Mossad operations of the 1960s and pioneered many of the tactics currently used by intelligence agencies worldwide, referenced recent terror attacks against Israel, Europe, and the United States; Iran's alleged nuclear ambitions; the insurgency in Iraq and Afghanistan; and worldwide Muslim riots.

"It looks to me like it is a kind of coordinated or contemplated problem to somehow impose the Islamic idea all over the world," Amit said.

Lesson #5: Land-for-peace formula is really a terrorist rouse

"The illegal Israeli occupation of the West Bank and East Jerusalem is the basis for the entire conflict. Once a peace agreement is signed and Israel gets out of our land, there will be peace," said a Palestinian official during a live segment on the Al Jazeera television network for which I was a guest commentator.

On air, I retorted Israel didn't recapture the West Bank or eastern sections of Jerusalem until the 1967 Six Day War, when Arab countries used those territories to launch an invasion into the Jewish state. Arab nations were initiating wars against Israel long before the West Bank and eastern Jerusalem fell into the Jewish state's hands. It's ridiculous to claim the basis of the Arab gripe with Israel is about particular pieces of territory.

I explained that when Iranian President Mahmoud Ahmadinejad states he wants to wipe Israel off the map, he doesn't single out any specific land but talks of the entire Jewish state. I explained how the Oslo Accords, in which Israel gave PLO Leader Yasser Arafat a fiefdom within rocket range of Israeli cities in exchange for promises of peace was an obvious total failure. Arafat used the territory gained to launch his *intifada* aimed at liberating Palestine by force.

I explained how Arafat's Palestinian National Council in 1974 adopted the "Phased plan," calling for the liberation of Palestine in stages and that Arafat routinely referred to this plan as his basis for accepting land-for-peace deals.

Still, the U.S., the Israeli government and most of the international community holds on to the notion that the land-for-peace formula works, that giving up strategic territory in exchange for a signed peace treaty is somehow the solution to the region's troubles.

I spoke to a top Hamas chief, who asked that his name be withheld, and he explained what he says his group has in mind when it comes to land-for-peace.

"The Muslim hero Saladin gave up land when he gave Acco to the Crusaders in order to keep Jerusalem," the Hamas chief told me. "Therefore, I say that the possibility of the exchange of territories existed already in the history of Islam and it cohabitates with our principle that all of Palestine is a dedicated land from Allah, may he be blessed to the Muslims, and no one has the right to give up any part of it."

He outlined for me a "peace deal" Hamas would accept in which Israel gives up land for Hamas's promises to end attacks.

"We will be ready for a long interim renewable agreement in which Israel gives land based on a period of cease-fire that can go to ten or even fifteen years like it was done by the prophet Muhammad with the enemies of the Muslims," said the senior Hamas official.

The Hamas leader said his group would offer Israel "temporary peace" in exchange for Israel vacating the West Bank, eastern Jerusalem, parts of the southern Israeli Negev desert that border the Gaza Strip, and the Jordan Valley, which extends from outside Jerusalem toward Jordan and encompasses most of Israel's major water supplies.

The Hamas chief said Israel would "be surprised" by his group's willingness to end attacks if only the Jewish state retreats from strategic land. He said a "peace agreement" was in Hamas's interests, explaining a deal with Israel would help his terror group garner international legitimacy and donor funds.

The Hamas leader, though, said his group will not abandon its goal of destroying Israel.

"When I speak about a long cease-fire and a temporary agreement, it means that we do not recognize the right of the state of the occupation on our lands, but we will accept its existence temporarily," said the leader.

The leader insisted any peace deal is based on the reality Hamas will not be able to defeat Israel in the near future, but he said his group is confident it ultimately will be "victorious."

"I do not see the Palestinian people and Islamic nation succeeding to liberate this blessed land of Palestine in the very near future," he said. "This is an Islamic land and the Jews are invited to live in Palestine and the Muslims will guaranty their safety and honor...But we will never give up our right for the whole of Palestine. We should be realistic to admit that the mission for the liberation of Palestine will pass on to the coming generations."

Even members of Palestinian Authority President Mahmoud Abbas's Fatah group—deemed "moderate" by the U.S.—told me any land for peace deal with Israel is only a temporary machination to further their goal of destroying the Jewish state.

Abu Ahmed, the Al Aqsa Martyrs Brigades leader and rocket commander in the northern Gaza Strip, told me when Abbas talks of land-for-peace it's "part of Abu Mazen's [Abbas's] political calculations due to commitments to the international community but we have not abandoned our fight of taking over all of Palestine."

The Brigades is the "military wing" of Fatah. Abu Ahmed said his group is "one and the same and totally a part of Fatah" and coordinates "resistance operations" with the Fatah party.

Regarding Abbas's peace talks, Abu Ahmed said, "Listen, we are aware of our president's [Abbas's] declarations but we are also aware of the international political system that brings the president to adopt this position."

Lesson #6: Mega-terror attacks like 9/11 "take time to prepare"

One thing I've heard a lot recently is that since there hasn't been another mega-terror attack in the U.S. since 2001 we must be doing something right. While we've made enormous advances in the war on terror, while our law-enforcement agencies have reportedly thwarted several planned major attacks, according to the terrorists we should not feel we are out of the woods yet. They claim another September 11 is on its way. It just takes time, they say.

Al Aqsa's Ramadan Adassi pointed out that "one should understand an attack, a big one like September 11, demands a lot of time to plan. Therefore, this is not the American occupation in Afghanistan and Iraq that is preventing the next attack, which I think is only a question of time."

He reminded me that while there hasn't yet been another mega-attack on the American home front, "still every day there are attacks in London, in Madrid, in Asia, in Afghanistan, in Iraq, and elsewhere."

Islamic Jihad's Abu Mosaab stated it's been a while since the last big home front attack "simply because an attack like 9/11 must be well prepared. I know that small attacks that the Palestinian resistance carries out like bombing attacks require lots of preparation and coordination, so imagine what preparation is required for such a big attack like September 11.

"It is for sure not the American efforts and measures that prevent it," he claimed. "In a world of almost seven billion persons it is hard to stop a cell of ten persons that somewhere in the world is preparing such an attack."

Abu Muhammad, a senior leader of the Al Aqsa Martyrs Brigades in the northern West Bank town of Jenin, told me the September 11 attacks were the "beginning of the collapse of the American empire," and it was only a question of time before the next "great big event" strikes the United States.

"Our nineteen heroes got the revenge of all the Muslims in the world and all the poor and exploited people and nations," he said.

"September 11 was a great day. The first minutes after the people understood what happened, Palestinians went out into the streets and started distributing candies and started hugging one another," he said. "Everybody felt that Allah gave us a present and that history will never be the same because Islam finally got rid of all the handcuffs that restricted and prevented it to express itself and its capacities."

Abu Muhammad warned the Quran has determined that another 9/11 is coming to America.

"In the Quran, it is written that the non-believers will destroy their homelands and their houses with their own hands. We are sure that Allah will help us defeat the Americans and collapse this empire," he said.

CHAPTER NINE

TERRORISTS GO GA-GA OVER HILLARY CLINTON

IF THIS PRESIDENT does not get us out of Iraq, when I am president, I will," pledged Senator Hillary Rodham Clinton in a televised Democrat primary debate broadcast nationally and around the world.

"The first day, I would get us out of Iraq by diplomacy," said New Mexico Gov. Bill Richardson, on the debate stage with seven other Democrat candidate hopefuls.

"We are one signature away from ending this war," declared Illinois Senator Barack Hussein Obama, stating if Bush won't change his mind about vetoing a bill requiring troop withdrawal, Democrats need to work on rounding up enough Republican votes to override him.

Former North Carolina Senator John Edwards, who together with Clinton and some others voted to authorize the Iraq war, apologized for his earlier support and said he wanted to see a withdrawal.

The primary debate, held in April 2007, was followed closely in the Middle East, where it was covered by Arabic news outlets and partially broadcast on major Arab satellite networks. Among those watching were Palestinian terrorist leaders, it turned out.

A lot of people tend to think terrorists live like barbarians in caves. Actually, a lot of terrorists, certainly those in the Gaza Strip and West Bank, reside in well-decorated apartments with all the trappings of a modern production company. They have some of the most advanced communications equipment in the world, some of it, in the case of Palestinian groups, reportedly supplied by Iran. As we discussed earlier, the terrorists are quite Internet-savvy, often conducting financial transactions online and using chat rooms and message boards to communicate and plot.

While terrorists spend a lot of time in the field carrying out or planning attacks or undergoing or leading military training, they also find the time to follow the news media closely. They need to. Being a terrorist is partially a political job. Many times attacks are perpetuated in response to the news cycle and the latest political developments, particularly in America. Also terror leaders understand very well how and when to issue statements and the rebound effects their words often have.

A good deal of the terror leaders I spoke to for this book understand some English, although they pretend not to and almost always demand we speak with the aid of an Arabic interpreter. They say they are not comfortable making pronouncements in English. I know they understand my English because during in-person talks, they have at times responded to my statements with gestures or laughter or disagreement before my words were translated for them into Arabic. Some of the terrorists speak almost fluent English, which they said they learned from watching American television networks, or, incredibly, in some cases from studying in Europe. Some Palestinian terrorists actually speak fluent Hebrew from time spent in Israeli jails. But the terrorists overwhelmingly get their news from very biased, anti-Western Arab sources in the Arabic language.

I was stunned by how closely some terrorists follow U.S. developments, how familiar they are with our political system and a lot of the top players. When the Democrats were victorious in the November 2006 midterm elections, the terrorists told me they noted the seeming changes in American attitudes regarding the war in Iraq and disappointment with the Bush administration.

And on this particular April day, the terrorists watched Arabic translations on Mideast news broadcasts of Democratic presidential hopefuls the night before flashing their antiwar credentials by competing with each other on who would withdraw from Iraq first.

The next day I happened to call Abu Jihad, one of the leaders of the Al Aqsa Martyrs Brigades terror organization in the terror stronghold of Nablus in the northern West Bank, for an article I was writing about Palestinian rocket capabilities. But out of the blue, during our interview, without any prompting on my part, Abu Jihad commented on how thrilled he was with the Democrat primary debate.

"We see Hillary [Clinton] and other candidates are competing on who will withdraw from Iraq and who is guilty of supporting the Iraqi invasion. This is a moment of glory for the revolutionary movements in the Arab world in general and for the Iraqi resistance movement specifically," said Abu Jihad. "I think Democrats will do good if they will withdraw as soon as they are in power."

Abu Jihad said he believes if elected to the White House, the Democrats will immediately order a withdrawal from Iraq. He warned if a retreat is not carried out, the U.S. will likely be attacked on the home front.

"The [Democrat] debate showed that like in Vietnam the American people needed these thousands of soldiers killed to see that invading other people will always result in a failure...I think the Democrats will win and apply an immediate withdrawal, but if they don't [withdraw], the revolutionary movements in Iraq will intensify attacks, and I think you should prepare for another big attack in the U.S."

Wow, I thought. A terrorist sounding off about a very specific American political debate. I quickly called one of Abu Jihad's bosses, Nasser Abu Aziz, the deputy commander of the Al Aqsa Martyrs Brigades in the northern West Bank. He too paid attention to the Democrat primary debate.

Abu Aziz said the debate proved "the invasion of Iraq was judged by Allah to be a failure. America needs to stop letting its foreign policy be dictated by the Zionists and the Zionist lobby. The Democrats understand this point and want to prevent this scenario."

He declared it is "very good" there are "voices like Hillary and others who are now attacking the Iraq invasion."

"I think the more Americans receive the bodies of soldiers killed in Iraq and Afghanistan, the more the conservatives in the U.S. will be sentenced to be thrown in the garbage," he said.

With America heading toward 2008 presidential elections, I talked with the terrorists about which parties they favor and who specifically they want to see in the White House.

Overwhelmingly they told me they hope Americans sweep the Democrats into power in part because of the party's position on withdrawing from Iraq, a move, as they see it, that ensures victory for the worldwide Islamic resistance.

"Of course Americans should vote Democrat," said Jihad Jaara, an exiled member of the Al Aqsa Martyrs Brigades terror group and the infamous leader of the 2002 siege of Bethlehem's Church of the Nativity.

"This is why American Muslims will support the Democrats, because there is an atmosphere in America that encourages those who want to withdraw from Iraq. It is time that the American people support those who want to take them out of this Iraqi mud," said Jaara, who talked to me from exile in Ireland, where he was sent as part of a deal that ended the church siege.

I asked the terrorists what they thought of statements from people like Senator Barbara Boxer and Representatives Barbara Lee and John Murtha that the U.S. must immediately withdraw from Iraq. What do they think when they hear prominent politicians comparing Iraq to Vietnam?

"These Democrat leaders are starting to ask the right questions: what are we doing in Iraq after we got rid from Saddam Hussein?" stated Jaara. "You succeeded in killing him and in establishing a new regime but why are you still there? And this is what these Democrats are asking. They understand that the American occupation causes the resistance and we are glad the resistance is succeeding to beat the Americans."

I must stop Jaara here and point out his deceptive rhetoric. When it suits them, terrorists claim American occupation of Iraq is the reason for their attacks. But terrorists have been waging their war for Islamic domination far before the U.S. diposed Saddam Hussein. September 11 occurred before the Iraq war. Jihadists constantly struggle to find new U.S. policies to blame for their terrorism.

Regarding the Democrat debate, Ala Senakreh, chief of the Al Aqsa Martyrs Brigades in the West Bank, said making statements is not enough, but Democrat policies make him hopeful.

"It is not enough to compare Iraq to Vietnam. There must be a big campaign to start this withdrawal. What is happening now in the congress is encouraging, it gives hope for a change, but I am afraid that it will still take time. As for us, this proves that the resistance always succeeds by the end of the day."

Abu Ayman, an Islamic Jihad leader in Jenin, said he is "emboldened" by those in America who compare the war in Iraq to Vietnam.

"[The *mujahedeen* fighters] brought the Americans to speak for the first time seriously and sincerely that Iraq is becoming a new Vietnam and that they should fix a schedule for their withdrawal from Iraq," boasted Abu Ayman.

Jihad Jaara said an American withdrawal would mark the beginning of the collapse of America.

"Therefore, a victory in Iraq would be a greater defeat for America than in Vietnam."

Jaara said vacating Iraq would also "reinforce Palestinian resistance organizations, especially from the moral point of view. But we also learn from these [insurgency] movements militarily. We look and learn from them."

Hamas's Abu Abdullah argued a withdrawal from Iraq would "convince those among the Palestinians who still have doubts in the efficiency of the resistance."

"The victory of the resistance in Iraq would prove once more that when the will and the faith are applied victory is not only a slogan. We saw that in Lebanon [during Israel's confrontation against Hezbollah there in July and August, 2006]; we saw it in Gaza [after Israel withdrew from the territory in 2005], and we will see it everywhere there is occupation," Abdullah said.

The terror leaders each independently urged American citizens to vote for Democratic candidates.

There has been some thinking when al-Qaida has in the past made statements that can be construed as somewhat negative toward Bush, some analysts speculated the terrorists really were trying to generate American support toward the U.S. president and his political party. Perhaps the terrorists here are doing the opposite—endorsing Democrats to ensure a Democrat defeat?

I can resoundingly reject that notion. Maybe such a thing can be argued regarding a well-planned, pre-written, thoroughly premeditated al-Qaida statement. But I have spoken to a large number of terrorists, many of whom didn't know what the topics of our interviews would be beforehand. I talked with terror leaders from competing organizations, who couldn't possibly orchestrate some sort of conspiracy to harm an American political party. And I have talked countless times off-the-record to terrorists about U.S. politics. And one hundred percent of the time the terror leaders favored the Democrats over the Republicans.

I never once came across a single terrorist who supported any Republican. And why would they? The Democrats largely want to withdraw from Iraq. They want dialogue with Syria and Iran. The terrorists share those same goals, because they believe it will lead to the downfall of the American empire and the spread of Islam. It was under a Democrat president, Bill Clinton, PLO leader Yasser Arafat returned from exile in Tunis, established a fiefdom in the West Bank and Gaza, and was built up as a legitimate leader, becoming the most frequent foreign dignitary to visit the White House. The terrorists love that. They believe the Democrats are their ticket to victory and they are hopeful a Democrat will soon sit in the Oval Office.

I asked them about particular presidential candidates. Overwhelmingly, the terrorists favored Hillary Clinton to win in 2008.

Brigades chief Ala Senakreh told me he "hopes Hillary is elected in order to have the occasion to carry out all the promises she is giving regarding Iraq.

"I hope also she will maintain her husband's policies regarding Palestine and even develop that policy. President Clinton wanted to give the Palestinians 98 percent of the West Bank territories. I hope Hillary will move a step forward and will give the

Palestinians all their rights. She has the chance to save the American nation and the Americans life."

Senakreh has planned and orchestrated multiple suicide bombings and has himself carried out at least a dozen shooting attacks against Israelis. He is heavily involved in all Brigades activities, and the Brigades is one of the most active Palestinian terror groups.

Abu Hamed, leader of the Al Aqsa Brigades in the northern Gaza Strip, explained Hillary's antiwar position "proves that important leaders are understanding the situation differently and are understanding the price and the consequences of the American policy in Iraq and in the world.

"The Iraqi resistance is succeeding. Hillary and the Democrats call for withdrawal. Her [Clinton's] popularity shows that the resistance is winning and that the occupation is losing. We just hope that she will go until the end and change the American policy, which is based on oppressing poor and innocent people."

Sure, Abu Hamed, American policy, which freed Iraqis from Saddam's brutal, tyrannical regime is based on oppressing innocents.

Hamed's terror cell is responsible for coordinating a lot of the rocket fire aimed from the northern Gaza Strip at nearby Jewish communities.

Ramadan Adassi, leader of the Al Aqsa Brigades in the Anskar refugee camp in the northern West Bank, said he too backs Hillary. He said he hopes Hillary continues the legacy of her husband regarding the Palestinians, calling Bill Clinton "pro-Israel but [he] understood that the Palestinians must live in their independent state like the other nations of the world."

With a straight face, Adassi said he was worried if Hillary defied Israel she will be brought down like her husband, claiming White House intern Monica Lewinsky really was an Israeli implant sent to lure Bill into a sex scandal after he pressured the Jewish state to evacuate territory to the Palestinians.

"If Hillary goes too much against the Zionist interests, she will face the same conspiracy like her husband who fell into the trap of Lewinsky. I have no doubt [Lewinsky] was planted by the

Zionists, who wanted to send a message to all future American presidents—do not go against the Israeli policy. Bill Clinton made the Oslo agreement and promoted peace but the Israelis did not give him a chance," Adassi said.

The theme of Lewinsky as an Israeli agent is commonly believed in the terror community. It came up many times in my conversations and interviews with Palestinian terrorists.

◇

The terrorists weren't familiar with the particulars of some of the other presidential hopefuls, but they all knew of former New York Mayor Rudy Giuliani. He is quite famous in terror circles for the time in 1995 he booted Yasser Arafat from an invitation-only concert at New York's Lincoln Center celebrating the United Nations fiftieth anniversary in New York with a glittering invite list of dignitaries and diplomats. Arafat attempted to crash the event. When Giuliani saw the PLO leader and his entourage making their way to a private box seat near the stage, the mayor immediately ordered Arafat off the premises.

The debacle occurred at the height of Oslo euphoria, when Arafat was being promoted as some sort of statesmen and even most mainstream Jewish groups disgracefully embraced the murdering terrorist. But Giuliani spurned Arafat, explaining his concerns came from his days as a Federal prosecutor, when he investigated terrorist incidents linked to Arafat.

"Giuliani doesn't deserve to live or even to be mentioned," said Brigades leader Ala Senakreh. "He wants war and he will most probably receive war. He hates Palestinians and we hate him. He hates Arafat and I tell him that it is Arafat who brought us to be very close to our independent state after decades during which Israel and your government did everything in order to prevent us from having our state."

Adassi threatened Giuliani:

"If I had the occasion to meet him I would hurt him. For the sake of the American people Giuliani shouldn't be elected. He is a disgusting guy and I think Americans must think very hard about their future and their soldiers who will be killed when they come to elect their leaders."

Abu Hamed blathered that Giuliani "can hate Arafat and the Palestinians, but he knows that nobody is hated in the world more than his leadership, his party, his president, and his Zionist friends. All the polls in the world prove that this [conservative] wing of America and the Zionists are considered to be the most dangerous for the security of the world."

Some of the terrorists were mildly familiar with Arizona Senator and Republican hopeful John McCain.

Senakreh called him a "stupid person. To you McCain I say this so-called war on terror you're promoting is causing only the loss of life of innocent people all around the world and the loss of your dog soldiers, and what is the result for you? Zero. Nothing."

The terrorists also sounded off about Barack Obama, who they said they had heard about from the Arab new media. They said they see him as some sort of crusader against Israel.

"I think Obama's success that I heard about in the media is an important success. He won popularity in spite of the Zionists and the conservatives, whom he greatly defeated. I think he can be a great leader but I don't think that the American regime will allow him to progress. They will try to get rid of him," stated Adassi.

I asked what he meant Obama "defeated" the conservatives and Israel. Adassi explained he was referring to Obama's strong anti–Iraq War stance.

While the terror leaders each independently urged American citizens to vote for Democratic candidates, not all believed the Democrats would actually carry out a withdrawal from Iraq. They believe most American politicians are controlled by Israel.

Islamic Jihad's Mahmoud Saadi stated, "Unfortunately I think those who are speaking about a withdrawal will not do so when they are in power and these promises will remain electoral slogans. It is not enough to withdraw from Iraq. They must withdraw from Afghanistan and from every Arab and Muslim land they occupy or have bases."

He called both Democrats and Republicans "agents of the Zionist lobby in the U.S."

Hamas's Abu Abdullah commented once Democrats are in power "the question is whether such a courageous leadership can [withdraw]. I am afraid that even after the American people will elect those who promise to leave Iraq, the U.S. will not do so. I tell the American people vote for withdrawal. Abandon Israel if you want to save America. Now will this happen? I do not believe it."

Hamas leader Muhammad Abu Tir, who was the number two Hamas terrorist in the newly formed Palestinian government, took it a step further and said not only the American government but also U.S. churches are controlled by the Jews.

Abu Tir, famous for his funny-looking orange-dyed beard, was arrested by Israel as part of its roundup of Hamas leaders in the summer of 2006. He is accused—and all but admitted to me he is guilty—of attempting to poison a Jerusalem restaurant and Israeli water supplies.

"Even the churches where the Americans pray are led by Jews who were converted to Christianity, but they were converted to keep controlling the Americans," said Abu Tir.

"I made a study and I know very well that all this radicalism in some parts of the Christianity, [including] the Evangelicals who are being led by Bush, is because of the control of Zionists," stated Abu Tir. The Hamas official went on to accuse "Zionists" of controlling Western media organizations and "leading terrorism inside the mass communications media."

The sheer poetry of it. A terrorist accusing others of terrorism.

I met Abu Tir at his palatial residence in eastern Jerusalem. During our interview, he basically physically assaulted me. As a habit, I often cross one of my legs over the other while conducting interviews. I learned from Abu Tir this position is considered a sign of disrespect in the Muslim world because it causes the shoe, which walks the lowly ground, to face the person next to you. Well, the first time I crossed my legs during our interview and my lowly shoe faced this strange-looking terrorist, Abu Tir pointed at my shoe and told me to stop. But I crossed my legs out of habit a second time and the orange-bearded terrorist lightly slapped my foot. Toward the end of our interview, I crossed my leg a third time, this time, I must admit, on purpose. I don't mind having my shoe face a terrorist. Abu Tir slapped my foot quite hard.

"I told you to stop that," he said in broken English, pointing his figure at me. "You need to learn."

"I'm sorry," I said. "I keep forgetting. It's out of habit."

I got off lightly. He could have poisoned me.

But Abu Tir, like the rest of the terrorists, agreed the Democrats are better than Bush's party.

One thing I learned early on is when interviewing terrorists not to give them an open microphone and ask what they think of Bush or the Republican Party. I just don't have the time or patience to listen to their never-ending tirades. It's better to ask pointed questions about specific Bush policies, although even then the terrorists digress into passionate, lengthy attacks on America's president, whom they despise more than pig fat.

"Bush is a sick person, an alcoholic person that has no control of what is going on around him," the Brigades Jihad Jaara told me.

Abu Hamed said he heard in the Arab news media one can speak with Bush seriously about politics for a maximum of half an hour, then Bush loses concentration and the guest must talk with him about golf.

"This proves that the American leaders are only the front of hidden leaders and interests that are now ruling America," Hamed told me.

Adassi called Bush "a psychopath, an arrogant person whose hands are full of blood of American soldiers in Iraq, American civilians killed on September 11, Palestinian, Iraqi, Afghani and other innocent children and women and innocent civilians. A stupid and insane person who will cause the loss even of America's allies in the Arab world."

The terrorists' deep-rooted hatred of Bush is, of course, to be expected. The man says he is trying to lead the war to eradicate terrorism. His declarations include destroying the very organizations whose leaders I interviewed. But I was surprised a lot of the terrorists I talked to were familiar with Republican leaders of the past, including President Ronald Reagan.

Lecturing me on American politics, Adassi explained Reagan was the political and ideological father of today's conservative movement and the doctrine the Bush administration has been advocating.

"I think Reagan can be considered the father of all these policies—responsible for the actual mess of America in the world. I hope for the American people that the winds of change we are seeing now in the Congress and the opposition to Bush in larger sections of American society prove the Reagan legacy was wrong," said Adassi.

"Americans are digesting now the price Reagan's ideology cost their country in the last few years," he said.

The terrorists also blasted former House Speaker Newt Gingrich. I read to them quotes from Gingrich and excerpts from some of his writings that I think very accurately encapsulate what he stands for. Even before that, many were familiar with his name. One surprised me by knowing some particulars of Gingrich's personal biography.

Gingrich has taken strong positions about defeating terror worldwide, pushing for strong military responses to terror.

Brigades chieftain Ala Senakreh called Gingrich a "Nazi."

"This Nazi must have personal economic interests and must be a very big opportunist, beside that he in person has no children and nothing to lose in this useless war against the rights of people to live in dignity without American and Israeli dictations. You, Nazi Gingrich, are promoting World War Three, and I am not sure that you will be the one who will win at its end."

Adassi deemed Gingrich a "pathetic demagogue. This sick man can be easily hospitalized with Bush in the same psychiatric hospital. His successes reflect the American stereotype that in the U.S. the more you are cruel and the more you are an assassin, the more you are popular."

"Before making all kinds of statements about Iraq, why doesn't this bastard look and see he is facing a military defeat in Iraq and soon a major defeat in the elections. If Gingrich is so courageous and so confidant, why did his devil party lose the [Midterm] elections?" Adassi declared.

That Nanci Pelosi is so Brave

"We came in friendship, hope, and determined that the road to Damascus is a road to peace," said a smiling, gloating Nancy Pelosi after emerging from a three-hour meeting with Syrian dictator Bashar Assad.

Pelosi, a Democratic senator from California who five months prior became House Speaker, flew to Syria in April 2007 to hold talks with President Assad in spite of fierce White House objection. American policy largely attempted to isolate Syria, which is seen as one of the most important state sponsors of terrorism. But breaking that isolation, Pelosi became the most senior U.S. official to visit Syria since Assad's regime was widely blamed for assassinating Lebanon's former Prime Minister Rafiq Hariri in 2005.

Assad signed a military alliance in 2004 with Iran, which is the largest supporter of terror worldwide and is suspected of seeking a nuclear weapons arsenal. Iran regularly ships rockets and all kinds of military supplies to Syria. Assad openly hosts the overall leaders of the Hamas and Islamic Jihad Palestinian terror groups. Israel says the Damascus-based leadership of those organizations routinely orders its operatives in the West Bank and Gaza Strip to carry out attacks, including suicide bombings, rocket firings, and shootings.

Syria openly backs the Lebanese Hezbollah militia and terrorist group and is accused of allowing large quantities of weapons to be transported from Syrian borders to Hezbollah, which last summer engaged in a war with the Jewish state.

Assad has been accused of supporting the insurgency against U.S. troops in Iraq; generating unrest in Lebanon, which his country military occupied for almost thirty years; and is accused of ordering the killing of Hariri. Assad's regime is routinely cited for human rights violations. It enforces tightly controlled rules requiring most aspects of civilian life to be coordinated with the government. The Syria media spews vicious anti-Semitic and anti-American propaganda.

And yet Pelosi saw fit to meet with Assad and call his country peaceful without Assad even making statements claiming he'll expel terror leaders or change his policies regarding Lebanon or Iran;

without Assad offering even cosmetic, meaningless gestures inching in the direction of allowing more freedom in his country.

Gordon Johndroe, a spokesman for President Bush's National Security Council, called Pelosi's trip "counterproductive" and said Damascus is "lined with the victims of Hamas and Hezbollah; the victims of terrorists who cross from Syria into Iraq."

Bush himself criticized Pelosi's visit, stating it sent "mixed messages" to the region and undermined U.S. policy.

"Photo opportunities and/or meetings with President Assad lead the Assad government to believe they're part of the mainstream of the international community," Bush told reporters in Washington. "In fact, they're a state sponsor of terror."

Pelosi is by far not the only U.S. political figure to visit Damascus since 2005 or meet with Syrian officials, but she was the most senior. The State Department quietly sent lower level diplomats to deal with such bureaucratic issues as population, refugees, and migration. Secretary of State Condoleezza Rice in May 2007 met briefly with her Syrian counterpart at a political convention in Iraq, but then resoundingly blasted Syria. To my information, the Bush administration sent representatives to Syria in 2006 to offer Assad a list of incentives to end his relationship with Iran and kick out Palestinian terror leaders, but the Syrian dictator didn't bite.

But Pelosi's visit, which included two lower profile Republicans, was a public gesture toward Assad. Some columnists and talk radio hosts in America blasted Pelosi for carrying out what they said was shadow diplomacy, creating a competing and contradictory U.S. policy that tows the line of many prominent Democrats and some Republicans who urge dialogue with Iran and Syria.

Pelosi's visit was widely covered by the pan-Arab media. The terrorists heard about it and they were ecstatic over Nancy.

"Nancy Pelosi understands the [Middle East] area well, more than Bush and Dr. [Condoleezza] Rice," said Khaled Al-Batch, the spokesperson of the Islamic Jihad terror organization, talking to me from Gaza one day after Pelosi's Syria trip.

"If the Democrats want to make negotiations with Syria, Hamas, and Hezbollah, this means the Democratic Party understands well what happens in this area and I think Pelosi will succeed...I hope she wins the next elections," Al-Batch said.

Al-Batch expressed hope Pelosi and the Democratic Party will pressure Bush to create dialogue with Syria and Middle East "resistance movements" and prompt an American withdrawal from Iraq.

"Bush and Dr. Rice made so many mistakes in the Middle East. Just look at Palestinian clashes and Iraq. But I think some changes are happening for the Bush administration's foreign policy because of the hand of Nancy Pelosi. I think the Democratic Party can do things the best...Pelosi is going down a good road by this policy of dialogue," he said.

"Pelosi's visit to Syria was very brave. She is a brave woman," Jihad Jaara of the Al Aqsa Martyrs Brigades terror group.

"I think it's very nice and I think it's much better when you sit face to face and talk to Assad. It's a very good idea. I think she is brave and hope all the people will support her. All the American people must make peace with Syria and Iran and with Hamas. Why not?" Jaara said.

Pelosi's visit emboldened some of America's enemies to believe the U.S. is cowering and on its way to defeat in the Middle East: Hamas "military wing" leader Abu Abdullah said the willingness by some lawmakers to talk with Syria "is proof of the importance of the resistance against the U.S."

"The Americans know and understand they are losing in Iraq and the Middle East and that their only chance to survive is to reduce hostilities with Arab countries and with Islam. Islam is the new giant of the world."

Syria provides refuge to the overall leader of Hamas, Khaled Meshaal, who often threatens the West from his safe haven in Damascus.

The boasting of Abu Abdullah and his ilk should not be taken as rhetoric. These terrorists are not being sensationalist. They watched an American politician coddle Assad and call him peace loving, and they smell weakness. They taste the beginnings of a change in U.S. attitudes.

George Galloway boots me for calling Hamas "terrorists"

The coddling of Mideast dictators and terror groups is, of course, not limited to American politicians. There are some leaders in the West who defend terrorism so fiercely they will openly side with the jihadists without even creating the pretense of "dialogue."

One such politician, extreme leftist British Member of Parliament George Galloway, actually kicked me out of his office and deployed the London police because I called Hamas a terrorist group! That's right. The same Hamas whose charter calls for the murder of Jews, the same Hamas that is responsible for scores of deadly suicide bombings, shooting attacks, and rocket firings into Jewish population centers.

Together with my occasional partner in crime, U.S. radio host Rusty Humphries, I interviewed Galloway in his London parliamentary offices in June 2007. Galloway is known for his controversial views against the war on Islamic terror and his fierce opposition to the state of Israel. He made several high-profile solidarity visits to Iraqi dictator Saddam Hussein and was friends with Arafat. He has defended Palestinian suicide bombings and has expressed support for Syria's previous occupation of Lebanon. The Scottish politician also has called President Bush and former Prime Minister Tony Blair "criminals." He even once told a magazine it would be "morally justified" to suicide bomb Blair.

Galloway has been embroiled in a U.S. and British investigation suspecting him of benefiting financially from the U.N. Oil for Food program. If indicted, he could lose his parliamentary seat.

My interview with Galloway was scheduled two weeks in advance through his assistant Kevin Ovenden, who was provided with the professional details for both myself and Rusty. I told Ovenden the interview would focus on Galloway's views regarding the war on terror in Iraq, Afghanistan, and Israel.

When we arrived in his small parliamentary office, Galloway was sitting at his computer smoking a fat cigar. Rusty, a cigar aficionado, commended Galloway on the politician's impressive collection.

"I don't have enough for everyone," Galloway snipped, even though Rusty didn't even imply he wanted a cigar.

I noticed Galloway's office was decorated with pictures of communist revolutionaries Fidel Castro and Che Guevara—along with dolls resembling Castro and Venezuelan president Hugo Chavez.

After introducing ourselves, we formally started the interview asking Galloway a few softball questions about his general feelings toward the war in Iraq. The entire interview and the ensuing drama was recorded using radio equipment.

Galloway called the Iraq war a "catastrophe" that "shattered Iraq as a society" and created "ten thousand new bin Ladens."

I asked Galloway whether he thinks Osama bin Laden is a terrorist. Galloway said the Al-Qaida chieftain is indeed a terrorist since bin Laden, whom he said was "armed and financed by the U.S." in the 1970s and 1980s, is a "pan-Islamic, nihilistic leader leading a nihilistic organization which seeks to bring about the collapse of national states and re-emergence of the caliphate."

But Galloway stated Hamas, by contrast, is not a terror group.

"[Hamas] wants to liberate their country, which has been illegally occupied, and to reassemble their nation, which has been scattered to the four winds. That's an entirely legitimate goal."

I tried to interject, explaining Hamas specifically targets civilians, which to me is the very definition of terrorism.

But Galloway cut me off, shouting, "Let me finish, please, because you're here obviously with an agenda, right down to the way you're holding the microphone as a kind of gun at my head."

Galloway, obviously annoyed that I disagreed with him, then argued that when it comes to determining who is a terrorist "what counts is not the firepower involved."

"You're not a terrorist because you've got X kind of weapons...you're a terrorist if your goals are illegitimate," he said. "And the goals of the national liberation movements of Palestine are entirely legitimate. And, I've got news for you, are widely supported around the world."

The issue, he said, is who is the target and what is the purpose of the "military action."

"A suicide bombing of a group of Israeli soldiers in illegal occupation of Palestinian lands is an entirely legitimate military act," Galloway said. "A suicide bombing of a group of Israeli settlers illegally occupying Palestinian land is an entirely justifiable military action. A suicide bombing of a falafel stall in Tel Aviv is not. A bombing of a nightclub in Haifa is not. So there's your answer."

Now Galloway got me really upset. I have good friends who are "Israeli settlers." This jihad-loving politician just called those friends legitimate targets.

I retorted by stating Hamas is not a local resistance movement but a terror group allied with the global jihad. Hamas leaders, including the group's chief in Gaza, Mahmoud Al-Zahar, featured in this book, regularly state they are seeking to impose a worldwide Islamic caliphate.

Galloway angrily asked me, "Is this an interview or a political broadcast on behalf of the Zionist movement?"

Sounding paranoid, he then lied:

"I didn't even know that you were coming here; you've actually got this interview under false pretenses."

"I most certainly did not," I responded, taken aback.

Not only did I coordinate the interview beforehand with Galloway's assistant Ovenden, but anyone who listens to the beginning of the recorded interview, which will be made readily available on the Internet, can hear Rusty and I discuss with Galloway exactly who we are.

Galloway quickly announced the end of the interview.

"I think that we should conclude this interview now. I told you at the beginning, before we started, I don't speak to the Israeli media."

"I'm not the Israeli media," I shot back, explaining I was a foreign correspondent based in Israel, which was exactly what I told Galloway's assistant two weeks prior and which is what I told Galloway at the start of our conversation.

"Well you might as well be [the Israeli media]. I have no intention of talking to either of you any further. So, good afternoon gentlemen," Galloway stated firmly, standing up and pointing to the door.

As I was gathering my equipment Galloway told Rusty and I to leave immediately or he would call the police. I was stupefied by that statement—what would he tell the police, that I called Hamas a terror group? So I laughed and invited Galloway to phone the police, not thinking he actually would.

Galloway then said, "I think I'm going to do exactly that before you leave." He then proceeded to call the parliamentary security team, who in turn dispatched the London police.

Not wanting to get into any trouble, Rusty and I rushed out of Galloway's office without realizing I had left my laptop and a bag with my personal items near his computer.

Galloway's assistant Ovenden escorted us into the elevator and down to the first floor lobby, where security is stationed. On the audio record, Ovenden can be heard telling Rusty and I, "Because you came in under false pretenses you won't set foot" in Westminster again.

Rusty and I repeatedly asked Ovenden to explain which false pretences he was referring to.

When we reached the lobby a team of security officers awaited us. We were told the London police were on their way. Ovenden proceeded to lie to the officers, claiming we entered Galloway's office "under false pretenses."

Rusty and I were told to wait in the lobby for the arrival of the police. Minutes later, a London officer detained and questioned us.

In a conversation caught on our tape, I asked the police officer what exactly we did wrong. The officer replied that according to Galloway's assistant Ovenden, after a few minutes my interview with Galloway came to a "question that wasn't something that perhaps they were expecting."

I replied, "But that isn't illegal."

"I'm not disagreeing with you, alright," the officer said, "but I know for a fact that somebody like Mr. Galloway, if he doesn't think the interview is going to be to his advantage, probably, is not going to want to speak to you."

When he confirmed Rusty and I were indeed members of the news media and not Zionist agents sent to infiltrate Galloway's offices, we were let go. But we were informed the police prepared an "intelligence report" on the incident. The officers explained to us that this didn't necessarily mean trouble for us but that our "personal details" and the Galloway incident would be made available to parliamentary security in association with any future visit.

On that note, Rusty and I departed the parliamentary office building. I told Rusty that I felt bad because he didn't get to talk much with Galloway. We had scheduled the interview for both my reporting and to conduct an interview for Rusty's radio show. Before we interviewed Galloway, the radio talker ironically had asked me to start the interview because he was certain I'd be nice. He was afraid if he began the interview, he'd piss off the Scottish politician and I wouldn't have a chance to talk.

Walking down the street, I soon realized I had left my laptop in Galloway's office.

I quickly phoned Galloway. A female assistant who had witnessed the entire ordeal answered. I requested to coordinate the return of my laptop. She replied, "Ha. I don't think so," and then abruptly ended the call.

Still recording the incident, Rusty and I ran back to the British parliamentary office building to a surprised security team and asked to file a report against Galloway for my stolen laptop. A security officer called Galloway's office about the return of my equipment. A few minutes later Ovenden emerged. Refusing to look at us, Galloway's assistant coldly placed my laptop on the floor, turned his back to us and departed without saying a word.

CONCLUSION

A JEW WHO BELIEVES in the present Torah is a non-believer who cannot be accepted into heaven. In order to enter heaven you should be Muslim," said Sheikh Salem Abu Muumen, a prominent religious leader in the northern West Bank city of Jenin.

"Jews are condemned to hell," he said.

Muumen, presented in Chapter Three, was the final terror interview I conducted for the book.

With his remarks about Judaism in tow, I departed Jenin and drove from the city of suicide bombers back to real life in Tel Aviv. Blasting Pearl Jam—I cannot drive in war zones without rock music—I passed through Jenin's final checkpoint feeling like Alice emerging from Wonderland. The world of terror is a fantasy island. Each man thinks his relationship with Allah justifies any conduct, any excuse, any lie. In the terror community night is day; antagonists are victims; women, senior citizens, and babies are military targets; reality and history are completely discarded in the most absurd of manners; and of course, Jews and Crusaders are the sources of all evil on earth.

Most of the Islamist arguments and conspiracies can be so easily deflated if anyone actually bothered to try. Their explanations, excuses and claimed justifications for *jihad* are ridiculous, but their lies are repeated so often we've come to believe them. We now accept as fact that the major gripes the global terrorists have with us are our troops in the Middle East and our support for Israel, when indeed their problem is our existence, our freedom, and our values, and the fact that we stand in the way of their creating an Islamic universe.

When you get down to it, the terrorists' lines of thinking are delusional. When terrorists tell me a targeted nightclub filled with teenagers really was a meeting place for Zionist and American secret service agents; or watermelons imported from Israel are infected with the AIDS virus to kill Muslims; or Jews secretly control Christianity and the world's churches as part of their plot for world domination, it's hard to talk to the *jihadists* with a straight face. These terrorists are not credible as adults. Not credible as leaders.

It would almost be impossible to take the terrorists seriously except that they are serious about spreading Islam through massacre and innocents worldwide are being murdered as a result.

People think the rules of terrorism are complicated, but talking with the terrorists the past few years I learned things are quite simple. If you hand over territory to terrorists bent on your destruction, they'll use the land to attack you. If you sign a ceasefire with the terrorists, they'll use the truce to rearm, regroup, and strengthen their forces to attack you. If you restrain your army when your country is at war with attacking terrorists, they will smell weakness and will attack you. If you provide weapons to terror groups, they'll use the arms to attack you.

If politicians call for concessions to terrorists and terror supporters, the terrorists will be emboldened and will attack you. If your media justifies terrorism and uses the terrorists' supposed grievances to legitimize *jihad*, the terrorists will be emboldened and will attack you. If your celebrities side with the enemy, if your people elect leaders hell-bent on accommodation with evil, the terrorists will believe they're winning and they will attack you.

As terrible as this may sound, I don't entirely blame the terrorists for their increased violence against us worldwide. I met our enemies. I stared into the eyes of men who carry out shootings and rocket attacks and send suicide bombers into civilian population centers. These people are pure evil. There is not an ounce of humanity in their bones. Their goal is our destruction. Nothing more. Nothing less.

When we present the terrorists with weakness, they would be fools not to exploit it. When we cower at their threats, when we retreat at their advances, when we restrain our troops during battle, when we announce we are "not winning," we are throwing raw meat at the global *jihad* monster and more Americans will die as a result.

While writing this book, while schmoozing with terrorists, one thing above all else was brought home to me repeatedly—with these people there is no room for negotiation or ideological modification. There is no room for reason. For Muhammad Abdel-El, Mahmoud al-Zahar, Ala Zenakreh and their comrades in Iraq, Afghanistan, Iran, Syria, the West Bank, Gaza, London, Madrid, and New York, this is a war to the finish. It's a war for our existence whether we admit it or not. And in such a war only one side can win.

INDEX

6

A

INDEX

INDEX

K

L

INDEX

Q

R

S

T

INDEX

Y

Z

INDEX

Y

Z